GREAT **HEALTHY** FOOD™
FOR
VEGETARIAN
KIDS

NICOLA GRAIMES

CARROLL & BROWN PUBLISHERS LIMITED

First published in 2002 in the United
Kingdom by:

Carroll & Brown Publishers Limited
20 Lonsdale Road
Queen's Park
London NW6 6RD

Managing Editor Becky Alexander
Editor Jessica Hughes
Managing Art Editor Emily Cook
Photographers David Murray
    & Jules Selmes
Food Stylists Clare Lewis & Kathy Mann

Copyright © 2002
Carroll & Brown Limited

A CIP catalogue record for this book is
available from the British Library.

ISBN 1-903258-31-6

Reproduced by RDC Tech Group, Malaysia
Printed and bound in Italy by Milano Stampa
First edition

The moral right of Nicola Graimes to be
identified as the author of this work has been
asserted in accordance with the Copyright,
Designs and Patents Act of 1988.

Contents

INTRODUCTION 4

1 Fresh Start 10

2 Light Bites 22

3 Packed Lunches 40

4 Main Meals 52

5 Sweet Treats 84

6 Let's Party 104

7 Drinks 118

RECIPE LIST AND
NUTRITIONAL ANALYSIS 124

INDEX 127

Introduction

It is widely accepted that what we eat in childhood has implications for our future health. What's more, eating habits are formed in the first few years, so it is essential for children to try and enjoy a wide variety of foods, encompassing a range of flavours, colours and textures. We all want good health for our children and this may be why you have chosen a vegetarian diet for your child. This book will enable you to feed your child a varied and nutritious diet, with recipes that will provide the foundations for good health way into adulthood.

The recipes in this book have been created to inspire and create an enjoyment of food. Many of us have the preconceived idea that children prefer bland, nursery food, but researchers have found that they are far more open to new and stronger flavours than previously thought. The recipes here take this into account – they are interesting and varied, as well as being simple to prepare. They range from snacks and packed lunches to more elaborate main meals and desserts, as well as fun party ideas. There are plenty of recipes that will appeal to children of all ages.

A BALANCED DIET

The key to good health is a well-balanced diet made up of a wide range of foods and this is entirely possible with a vegetarian diet. The following food groups should form the building blocks of your child's diet:

Fruits & Vegetables Whether fresh or frozen, fruits and vegetables are a crucial part of a child's diet, providing valuable vitamins, minerals and fibre. Leafy green vegetables, for example, are a good source of iron and should be a regular part of a vegetarian menu. (Other iron-rich foods include free-range

THE VEGETARIAN SOCIETY

This is the oldest vegetarian organisation in the world and is the leading voice and authority on vegetarianism. The society promotes the advantages of a vegetarian diet and aims to increase the number of options available to vegetarians through campaigning, educating, research and working with the food industry. The Vegetarian Society's symbol (as featured on the front cover of this book) is widely recognised as the most trusted guarantee of vegetarian suitability – it appears on thousands of food products and helps to take the guesswork out of shopping for vegetarian-friendly food. All of the recipes featured in this book are suitable for vegetarians and have been approved by The Vegetarian Society. For more information visit www.vegsoc.org

eggs, beans, lentils, fortified breakfast cereals, wholegrains and dried fruits, especially apricots. Consuming foods rich in vitamin C, such as a glass of orange juice at the same meal, will aid iron absorption.) It can be a battle to get children to eat vegetables, but try to offer around five different types a day. Presenting vegetables in various guises, such as puréed into soups and sauces, combined with mashed potato, in burgers, or dipped in humous or garlic butter, is a useful ploy.

Cereals & Grains These provide plenty of energy as well as valuable vitamins, minerals and fibre, and should form the main part of a meal. Wholegrains and brown rice provide the richest source of nutrients, but should not be given in large quantities to young children (under 5 years) due to their high fibre content. Babies and young children can find fibre difficult to digest in large quantities – too much may lead to stomach upsets and loss of appetite, so offer wholegrains in moderate amounts. This group also includes pasta, potatoes and (low-sugar) breakfast cereals.

Be Careful With . . .

It is always advisable to check product labels for non-vegetarian ingredients when buying foods. Vegetarian versions of most foods are now widely available, but you may want to check the following:

Additives – some colours, stabilizers and emulsifiers which may or may not be vegetarian. The most common are E120 (cochineal) and E441 (gelatine) both made from animal sources.

Animal fats – sometimes found in biscuits, ready-meals, ready-made pastry, stock, chips, margarine and ice cream. 'Edible fats' can mean animal fats.

Cheese – look for cheese with a vegetarian symbol, since some are made with animal rennet (an enzyme taken from the stomach of a calf). Non-vegetarian cheese is often used in pesto, sauces and ready-meals, so you may find it easier to make your own.

Chocolate – may contain whey and emulsifiers.

Eggs – if possible, try to buy organic, free-range eggs. Remember that some foods, such as mayonnaise or pasta, may contain battery-farmed eggs.

Jelly – usually contains animal-derived gelatine. Instead, look for products set with agar or guar gum.

Margarine – may contain animal fats, whey, gelatine and animal-derived vitamin D_3 and E numbers.

Soups and sauces – watch out for animal-based stocks.

Suet – look for vegetarian versions.

Sweets – may contain gelatine or cochineal.

Worcestershire sauce – most brands contain anchovies, but vegetarian versions do exist.

Yogurt, crème fraîche, fromage frais and ice cream – some low-fat varieties may contain gelatine.

Eggs, Beans & Nuts These foods, along with tofu, seeds, lentils and peas, are a good source of protein, essential for growth, development and repair. Since children grow so quickly, it is important they are given a protein food at every meal, but it is vital to offer a variety. If you can, buy organic, free-range eggs and make sure that they are well-cooked. Do not give whole nuts to children under five years old – they should be ground or chopped to avoid the risk of choking. If anyone in your family has an allergy of any kind, consult your doctor before introducing nuts to your child's diet.

Dairy Foods Vegetarian cheese, milk and yogurt provide essential protein, fat, vitamins and minerals, including calcium which is vital for healthy bones and teeth. Cow's milk can be used in cooking for babies from six months but do not give as a drink before one year. Whole milk is recommended before the age of five, since it provides the calories a growing child requires. If your child is a good eater, then semi-skimmed milk can be introduced from age two, if this is what your family prefer.

Fats A certain amount of fat is important for children because it provides a concentrated source of energy. There are, however, good and bad fats: saturated and hydrogenated fats found in cream, margarine, butter and many processed foods should only be eaten in small amounts. Polyunsaturated fats and monounsaturated fats found in nuts, seeds, vegetable and olive oil are preferable.

Salt Avoid adding salt to cooking before the age of one year, since a baby's kidneys are too immature to cope. Salt is found in most processed foods, often in surprisingly large quantities, so try to avoid these or look for low-salt varieties.

 FIRST FOODS

Until your child can eat the same food as the rest of the family (at around 12 months), new foods should be introduced gradually, depending on his or her age. In this book, recipes that are suitable for babies are marked with a star and with '6 to 8 months', '8 months to 1 year' and '1 year to 18 months'. Changes to ingredients or method are indicated, if necessary, for particular age groups. Here are some guidelines for when to introduce certain foods and which foods to avoid:

6 TO 8 MONTHS
Serve coarsely puréed, mashed or minced food
Foods to add to diet Dairy foods such as yogurt, milk puddings and cheese (in small amounts at first), cow's milk (in cooking), wheat, well-cooked eggs, tofu, lentils, beans, lightly spiced food, smooth peanut butter and finely ground nuts and seeds (as long as there is no history of nut allergies in the family)
Foods to avoid Cow's milk (as a drink), whole nuts, soft or blue cheese, raw eggs, salt, chillies, honey and sugar (small amounts are okay)

8 MONTHS TO 1 YEAR
Serve mashed, minced or chopped foods
Foods to add to diet Cheese, pulses and beans may be eaten in larger amounts atthis age
Foods to avoid Cow's milk (as a drink), whole nuts, soft or blue cheese, salt, raw eggs, chillies, honey and sugar (small amounts are okay)

1 YEAR TO 18 MONTHS
Serve chopped foods
Foods to add to diet Your child should now begin to eat the same food as the rest of the family
Foods to avoid Whole nuts, chillies and raw eggs

Sugar Try to avoid giving your child too many sweet foods and drinks, which can encourage a sweet tooth, leading to tooth decay. Three times a day is a sensible limit. Try to offer natural sources of sugar, such as fresh and dried fruit. Do not give honey to babies under one year, since it is high in sugar and there is a small risk of botulism poisoning, but it is fine for older children.

Drinks Sugary, fizzy drinks and squashes are best avoided. Drinks containing artificial sweeteners are no better, since the sweeteners have been found to cause hyperactivity and stomach upsets if consumed in large quantities. Instead offer water (boiled, cooled water to babies under one year) or diluted fruit juices.

BEFORE YOU COOK
The recipes featured in this book have been devised for children aged 12 months and over. If you are cooking for a child under 18 months, see the guidelines in the box on page 7. Remember that children vary greatly in their development and some younger children may enjoy food intended for their elders.

Parents are encouraged to use their initiative – you know what's best for your child.

Butter should be unsalted, vegetable stock low-salt and fruit juice unsweetened. Portion sizes vary depending on the meal or snack, but the main meals serve four (two adults and two children), unless otherwise stated. These are again guidelines, since appetites vary as much as children do.

Allergies Life-threatening allergies are very rare, but many would argue that the number of children suffering from food intolerance is on the increase. The foods that most commonly cause adverse reactions include cow's milk, eggs, wheat, tomatoes, strawberries, citrus fruit, nuts, sugar and artificial additives. If there is any history of food allergies in the family, or if you are concerned about a particular food, talk to your health visitor or doctor.

1 Fresh Start

It is now known that children who eat a good breakfast perform better at school and have improved concentration. This chapter features ideas for healthy, energy-packed breakfasts to give your kids the best possible start to the day.

BREAKFAST MAIL

This is cinnamon toast with a twist. To make breakfast-time more fun, put the initials of your child on the toast before cooking.

2 slices wholemeal or white bread

Small knob of butter

½ teaspoon ground cinnamon

½ teaspoon caster sugar

Serves 1

8 MONTHS TO 1 YEAR
Cinnamon toast is suitable for your baby; cut it into fingers before serving.

1 Preheat the grill to high. Using a sharp knife or scissors, cut out your child's initial(s), or name if it is short, from one slice of bread. Dampen the letter(s) with water and place on the other slice of bread, damp-side down. Press down the shape to make it stick.

2 Toast the bread, with the shape-side facing up, until golden. Turn the bread over and toast the other side.

3 While the bread is toasting, mix together the butter, cinnamon and sugar. Spread the mixture over the shape side and serve immediately.

EGGY BREAD

For added appeal, cut the bread into shapes before dipping it into the egg.

1–2 slices wholemeal or white bread

1 free-range egg, beaten

Splash of milk

Butter, for frying

Serves 1

1 Using scissors or pastry cutters cut the bread into triangles or other shapes.

2 Mix the egg and milk together in a wide, shallow bowl and dip the bread into the mixture.

3 Heat some butter in a heavy-based frying pan. Place the bread in the pan and cook, turning once, until the egg has set and is golden. Serve immediately. This can be served on its own or with grilled tomato or baked beans for a more substantial breakfast.

Sweet Eggy Bread To make sweet eggy bread, sprinkle the bread with soft brown sugar and ground cinnamon just before serving.

EGG CUPS

Baby brioche are great for filling with all manner of sweet and savoury goodies. Scrambled egg makes a great filling and is also a good source of iron and protein, making it ideal for a vegetarian diet.

1 Preheat the oven to 140°C, gas mark 1. Wrap the brioche in foil and warm in the oven while you make the egg filling.

2 Meanwhile, heat the butter in a heavy-based saucepan. When it has melted, add the beaten eggs. Using a wooden spoon, stir continuously to prevent them sticking. When the egg is semi-solid, creamy and well scrambled, remove the pan from the heat – the egg will continue to cook in the heat from the pan.

3 Slice off the top of the brioche and scoop out the centre to make a cup. Spoon the scrambled egg into the middle and sprinkle with the chives. Replace the lid of the brioche before serving.

1 small brioche

25 g butter

2 free-range eggs, beaten

Few snipped chives, to garnish

Serves 1

6 TO 8 MONTHS
Make sure the egg is well cooked. You may want to cut the brioche into strips before serving.

MELTED CHOCOLATE & BANANA CROISSANT

1 croissant

25 g milk chocolate, grated, or chocolate spread

½ small banana, sliced

Serves 1

Warm croissant, gooey chocolate and soft banana – what could make a more delicious start to the day? This is a definite favourite with kids and a treat for mums and dads too.

1 Preheat the oven to 150°C, gas mark 2. Split the croissant lengthways, without cutting it completely in half.

2 Sprinkle the grated chocolate inside the croissant, reserving a little for the top, or cover the inside with chocolate spread. Arrange the banana on top of the chocolate and press the top half of the croissant down. Sprinkle grated chocolate (if using) over the top.

3 Place the croissant on a baking sheet and cook for 10–15 minutes until the chocolate has just melted and the croissant is warmed through.

Cheese & Tomato Croissant *Preheat the oven to 150°C, gas mark 2. Split the croissant lengthways and sprinkle with 25 g grated vegetarian Cheddar cheese, reserving a little for sprinkling on top. Arrange slices of tomato on top of the cheese and press the top of the croissant down. Sprinkle with the reserved cheese and place on a baking sheet. Bake for 10–15 minutes until the cheese has melted.*

TROPICAL FRUIT CRUNCH

This muesli couldn't be easier to make and is packed with healthy nuts, seeds and fruit. You can vary the dried fruit you use, for a change. It will keep for 14 days in an airtight container.

1   Toast the almonds, pumpkin and sunflower seeds in a dry frying pan over a medium heat for about 3 minutes, stirring frequently until golden.

2   Combine the toasted nuts and seeds with the rest of the ingredients and mix well. Transfer to an airtight container and store until ready to eat. Serve with milk and fresh fruit, if you like.

55 g flaked almonds

55 g pumpkin seeds

55 g sunflower seeds

115 g barley flakes

115 g porridge oats

140 g wheat flakes

55 g desiccated coconut

175 g raisins

175 g ready-to-eat dried apricots, roughly chopped

85 g dried pineapple slices, roughly chopped

Makes about 15 servings

6 TO 8 MONTHS
Soak a small serving of the muesli in breast, formula or cow's milk until softened. Purée until almost smooth.

YOGURT & BANANA MUNCH

This simple breakfast looks pretty if arranged in layers in a tall glass. Any type of fresh fruit can be used instead of the banana and it is a useful way of increasing the amount of fruit in your child's diet.

Arrange three-quarters of the banana in the bottom of a tall glass. Top with half of the yogurt, followed by a layer of the Golden Granola. Spoon the rest of the yogurt over the granola and decorate with the remaining banana. Spoon the honey on top before serving.

½ banana, sliced

100 g live, natural bio yogurt

4–6 tablespoons Golden Granola (see recipe page 16) without the dried fruit, or a similar crunchy breakfast cereal

1 teaspoon clear honey

Serves 1

6 TO 8 MONTHS
Make the granola a few hours before serving to allow it to soften. Honey is not recommended for babies under 1 year, so omit from this recipe.

GOLDEN GRANOLA

Many commercial breakfast cereals contain unwanted additives and are often laden with sugar. With this recipe you can decide on which ingredients you use and include your favourite nuts, grains and fruits. It will keep for 14 days in an airtight container.

1 Preheat the oven to 140°C, gas mark 1. Place the hazelnuts in a plastic bag and crush with a rolling pin until broken roughly. Put the hazelnuts, oats, barley, almonds and sesame and sunflower seeds in a bowl and mix well.

2 Heat the oil and honey in a saucepan over a medium heat. Stir the honey mixture into the nuts and grains and mix well.

3 Spoon the nut and grain mixture in an even layer onto 2 baking sheets and bake in the oven for 45 minutes, stirring occasionally, until golden and slightly crisp (the mixture will become more crispy as it cools).

4 Transfer the mixture to a large mixing bowl and add the banana chips, apricots and raisins. Mix well and allow to cool. Store in an airtight container until ready to eat. Serve with milk and fresh fruit, if you like.

---

55 g whole hazelnuts

115 g porridge oats

85 g barley flakes

55 g flaked almonds

55 g sesame seeds

55 g sunflower seeds

50 ml sunflower oil

5 tablespoons clear honey

55 g banana chips, broken

85 g ready-to-eat dried apricots, roughly chopped

85 g raisins

Makes about 10 servings

6 TO 8 MONTHS
Omit the honey. Grind the cereal until finely chopped. Chop the dried fruit into small pieces. Soak the mixture in breast, formula or cow's milk before serving.

PORRIDGE WITH APRICOT PUREE

Goldilocks would definitely have approved of this creamy porridge topped with puréed apricots, honey and nutmeg.

1   To make the apricot purée, place the apricots in a saucepan and cover with the water. Bring to the boil, cover the pan, then reduce the heat and simmer for 30 minutes until the apricots are very tender. Place the apricots, along with any water left in the pan, in a blender or food processor and purée until smooth.

2   To make the porridge, put the oats and bran (if using) into a saucepan. Add the milk and bring to the boil, stirring occasionally. Reduce the heat and simmer, stirring frequently, for 4 minutes until smooth and creamy.

3   Serve the porridge in a bowl, topped with a large spoonful of apricot purée, a spoonful of honey and a sprinkling of nutmeg.

FOR THE APRICOT PUREE

115 g ready-to-eat dried apricots

300 ml water

FOR THE PORRIDGE

55 g porridge oats

1 teaspoon bran (optional)

125 ml milk

1 teaspoon clear honey, to serve

Freshly grated nutmeg, to serve

Serves 1 (apricot purée serves 4)

6 TO 8 MONTHS

This porridge is suitable for your baby and can be made with formula milk, if necessary. Stir the apricot purée into the porridge, but omit the honey.

APRICOT & PRUNE FRUIT SPREAD

Many jams have a surprisingly low fruit content and are high in added sugar. This healthier alternative is much better for you and your children, and is an excellent source of vitamins and minerals.

1   Put the apricots and prunes in a non-metallic saucepan. Cover with 425 ml of the water and bring to the boil. Reduce the heat, cover, and simmer for 45 minutes until the fruit is very soft, swollen and almost caramelised.

2   Transfer the cooked fruit to a blender or food processor and blend with the remaining water to make a thick purée. Spoon the fruit spread into an airtight jar or container and store in the refrigerator for up to a week.

115 g ready-to-eat dried apricots

115 g ready-to-eat dried prunes

500 ml water

Makes 350 g

6 TO 8 MONTHS

This spread is very high in fibre, so only give to babies in moderate amounts. Spread thinly on bread or add a teaspoonful to natural yogurt.

SPICED APPLE PUREE

This apple purée includes a delicious hint of cloves and cinnamon. It can be served with yogurt for breakfast and also makes a perfect base for apple crumble.

4 medium dessert apples, peeled, cored and roughly diced

150 ml exotic fruit juice or apple juice

1 teaspoon ground cinnamon

2 cloves

1 teaspoon vanilla extract

1 tablespoon soft brown sugar

15 g butter

Serves 2

1 Place the apples in a heavy-based, non-metallic saucepan with the fruit juice, cinnamon, cloves, vanilla and sugar. Cook, half-covered, over a medium heat for 20 minutes, until the apples are tender.

2 Remove the cloves and stir in the butter to make a rich sauce. Serve with natural yogurt or fromage frais.

AMERICAN-STYLE PANCAKES WITH MAPLE BANANAS

This breakfast is a real winner with children. If you don't have any maple syrup, honey is equally tasty, while slices of peach or nectarine make a delicious alternative to the bananas.

FOR THE PANCAKES

140 g plain flour, sifted

Pinch of salt

2 tablespoons caster sugar

1 teaspoon baking powder

1 free-range egg, beaten

300 ml buttermilk

125 ml milk

25 g butter, melted

Sunflower oil, for frying

FOR THE MAPLE BANANAS

2 tablespoons butter

4 tablespoons maple syrup

2 medium bananas, thickly sliced

Serves 4 (makes 10 pancakes)

1 Mix the flour, salt, sugar and baking powder together in a large bowl.

2 Mix together the egg, buttermilk, milk and butter, then add it to the flour mixture. Beat well to remove any lumps, making a thick batter.

3 Heat 1 teaspoon of oil in a large, heavy-based frying pan. Place 2 heaped tablespoons of batter per pancake in the hot oil – you will probably be able to cook 3 pancakes at a time. Cook the pancakes for 3 minutes until the base is golden, then turn them over and cook for a further 2 minutes. Place on a plate, covered with foil, to keep warm while you make the remaining pancakes.

4 Meanwhile, make the maple bananas. Melt the butter in a clean frying pan, add the maple syrup and cook for 2 minutes until slightly thickened. Add the bananas and cook, over a medium heat, for 1–2 minutes until softened.

5 To serve, spoon the bananas and maple syrup over the pancakes.

SUNSHINE RICE

This lightly spiced kedgeree makes a perfect Sunday brunch – high in carbohydrates and protein, it provides sustained amounts of energy for the day ahead. It also makes a great supper dish.

1 Put the lentils in a saucepan and cover with cold water. Bring to the boil, skim off any foam, then reduce the heat. Cover and simmer for 20–25 minutes until tender. Drain thoroughly.

2 Meanwhile, put the rice in a saucepan and cover with 450 ml cold water. Add the bay leaf (if using) and bring to the boil. Cover, reduce the heat and cook for 15 minutes until all the water has been absorbed and the rice is tender. Remove the bay leaf and set aside.

3 Melt the butter in a large, heavy-based frying pan, then add the curry powder and turmeric. Cook for 1 minute, stirring continuously.

4 Stir the lentils and rice into the butter and heat through.

5 Serve topped with the boiled egg and spring onion (if using).

---

50 g lentils, rinsed

225 g basmati rice, rinsed

1 bay leaf (optional)

50 g butter

1–2 teaspoons mild curry powder

½ teaspoon ground turmeric

4 free-range, hard-boiled eggs, quartered, to serve

1 spring onion, green part only, finely shredded, to garnish (optional)

Serves 4

Spinach Sunshine Rice *Boost the iron content of this dish by adding a handful of shredded fresh spinach leaves with the spices in Step 3. Cook for 2 minutes until the spinach is wilted and tender.*

6 TO 8 MONTHS
Use just 1 teaspoon of mild curry powder and blend the rice mixture until fairly smooth. Mash a well-cooked egg into the mixture.

BREAKFAST BUBBLE & SQUEAK CAKES

Any leftover vegetables can be used to make these delicious potato cakes and they are a perfect way to encourage children to eat cabbage! Peas, carrots, green beans and onion can also be used and a handful of grated Cheddar cheese mixed into the potato mash tastes great. Serve with grilled tomatoes, baked beans or a dollop of ketchup.

1   Cook the potatoes in plenty of boiling salted water for 15 minutes, or until tender. Drain well and mash until smooth.

2   Meanwhile, steam the cabbage for 5 minutes, or until tender, then slice into tiny pieces.

3   Combine the potatoes and cabbage with the mustard, spring onions (if using) and egg in a bowl. Mix well with a wooden spoon and leave to cool.

4   Shape the mixture into 8 cakes. Dust each cake with flour until well coated.

5   Heat 1 tablespoon of oil in a heavy-based frying pan. Fry 4 of the cakes over a medium heat for 3–4 minutes on each side, until golden, then repeat with the remaining cakes.

675 g potatoes, diced

175 g Savoy cabbage, finely shredded

1 tablespoon Dijon mustard

2 spring onions, finely chopped (optional)

1 free-range egg, beaten

Flour, for dusting

2 tablespoons vegetable oil, for frying

Serves 4

6 TO 8 MONTHS
Leave out the egg and spring onions, and serve as a mash. Add a little milk to make a smooth mixture.

Light Bites

2

This chapter offers a wide variety of tasty, nutritious ideas for snacks and light meals that are suitable for any time of day. Most of the recipes, such as the soups and dips, can be made in advance and served when required.

GREEN GIANT SOUP

This vibrantly coloured pea soup is a rich source of vitamin C – this enhances the absorption of iron, which is found also in peas.

1 tablespoon vegetable oil

1 medium leek, finely sliced

1 medium stick celery, finely chopped

225 g potato, diced

1 litre vegetable stock

280 g frozen petits pois

A few strips of cooked vegetarian bacon or 25 g vegetarian Cheddar cheese, grated, to serve

Serves 4

1 Heat the oil in a large, heavy-based saucepan. Add the leek and fry over a medium heat for 5 minutes until softened. Add the celery and potato and cook for a further 5 minutes.

2 Pour the stock over the vegetables and bring to the boil. Cover, reduce the heat and simmer the soup for 15 minutes. Add the petits pois and cook for a further 5 minutes until the potato is tender.

3 Using a hand-blender or food processor, blend the soup until smooth. Reheat the soup, if necessary, before serving and top with vegetarian bacon or Cheddar cheese.

LEEK, POTATO & SWEETCORN CHOWDER

Wonderfully creamy and filling, this classic soup looks attractive served San Francisco-style in a large, hollowed out crusty roll.

25 g butter

1 tablespoon sunflower oil

2 medium leeks, finely sliced

450 g potatoes, diced

600 ml milk

425 ml vegetable stock

400 g can unsweetened, reduced-salt sweetcorn, drained

2–3 tablespoons double cream (optional)

1 large bread roll, to serve

Few snipped chives, to garnish

Serves 4

1 Heat the butter and oil in a large, heavy-based saucepan. When the butter has melted, add the leeks and fry over a medium heat for 5 minutes until softened. Add the potatoes and cook for a further 5 minutes.

2 Add the milk and stock to the pan and bring to the boil. Reduce the heat and simmer, half-covered, for 10 minutes. Add the sweetcorn and simmer for a further 10 minutes, stirring occasionally, until the potatoes are tender.

3 Scoop out half of the vegetables and set aside. Purée the soup until smooth and creamy and return it, along with the rest of the vegetables, to the pan. Stir in the cream (if using) and heat gently.

4 Cut the top off the roll, then scoop out the inside, leaving a 1 cm-thick shell. Pour the soup into the bread roll and serve sprinkled with chives.

6 TO 8 MONTHS

Use water instead of vegetable stock to reduce the salt content of the dish.

SPICY CARROT & LENTIL SOUP WITH GARLIC CROUTONS

Mild spices add a pleasant warmth to this nutritious soup.

1 Heat the oil in a large, heavy-based saucepan. Add the onion, cover the pan and fry for 10 minutes over a low-medium heat until softened. Add the celery, carrots and spices, then cook for a further 3 minutes.

2 Add the lentils and cook for 1 minute, then stir in the stock. Bring to the boil, skim off any foam created by the lentils, then reduce the heat. Half-cover the pan and simmer for 35–40 minutes until the lentils are soft.

3 Using a food processor, blend the soup until smooth.

4 To make the croutons, rub the slices of bread with the garlic clove. Cut into cubes and place in a plastic bag with the olive oil. Shake until the cubes are coated in the oil, then fry over a medium heat until golden.

5 Serve the soup in bowls, with a spoonful of yogurt (if using) and sprinkle with the croutons.

FOR THE SOUP

1 tablespoon sunflower or vegetable oil

1 large onion, finely chopped

1 medium stick celery, finely chopped

4 medium carrots, finely sliced

1 teaspoon ground turmeric

1 teaspoon ground cumin

1–2 teaspoons mild curry powder

175 g red lentils, rinsed

1.2 litres vegetable stock

Plain yogurt, to serve (optional)

FOR THE GARLIC CROUTONS

2 slices day-old bread, crusts removed

1 garlic clove

1–2 tablespoons olive oil

Serves 4

NOODLE SOUP

This soup couldn't be easier to make – in fact, it's a bit of a cheat because it's made with instant miso soup with a few added extras. Nori is a type of seaweed that is full of nutritious minerals. You can find it in large supermarkets or health food shops. Cubes of marinated tofu also make a good addition to this soup.

1   Make the miso soup, following the manufacturer's instructions.

2   Meanwhile, cook the noodles in plenty of boiling water following the manufacturer's instructions. Add the beans and half of the carrots to the noodles 3 minutes before the end of the cooking time. Cook until tender, then drain well.

3   Place the noodles, carrots and beans in a serving bowl. Add the spinach and nori pieces (if using). Pour the hot miso soup over the top. Stir in the soy sauce.

4   Serve the soup garnished with the remaining carrot, spring onion and sesame seeds (if using).

2 sachets instant miso soup powder

125 g vegetarian noodles

25 g fine green beans, sliced

1 small carrot, finely shredded or cut into small shapes

Handful of fresh spinach leaves, shredded

2 toasted nori strips, broken into small pieces (optional)

1–2 teaspoons soy sauce

1 spring onion, finely shredded

Sesame seeds, toasted, to garnish (optional)

Serves 2

CHEESE & GRAPE BRUSCHETTA

Children will love these slices of cheesy baguette, which make a quick and nutritious snack. Sticks of celery make a good accompaniment.

1 Preheat the grill to high. Brush each side of the baguette slices with the oil and grill until golden.

2 Sprinkle each slice of baguette with the cheese and arrange the grapes on top. Grill the baguette for about 2 minutes until the cheese has melted. Serve immediately.

2–3 slices baguette

2 teaspoons olive oil

40 g vegetarian Cheddar cheese, grated

4 grapes, halved

Serves 1

TORTILLA PARCEL

A great alternative to the usual cheese sandwich. Use any fillings you have to hand and serve with slices of carrot and cucumber.

1 Place the mozzarella in the centre of the tortilla. Top with the tomato and the pesto. Fold in the sides of the tortilla to make a square parcel.

2 Heat the oil in a heavy-based frying pan with a lid. Place the parcel seam-side down in the frying pan. Cover the pan and fry over a low heat for about 3 minutes, turning once, until golden. Cut diagonally and serve.

2 slices vegetarian mozzarella

1 soft tortilla

2 slices tomato

1 teaspoon vegetarian pesto (see recipe page 60)

1 teaspoon olive oil

Serves 1

TORTILLA EGG ROLLS

This is scrambled egg with a twist. Flavoured with sun-dried tomato and spring onion, the egg is served in a warm rolled tortilla.

1 Preheat the oven to 140°C, gas mark 1. Heat the butter and oil in a heavy-based saucepan, add the pepper, spring onion and sun-dried tomatoes. Cook for 5 minutes until softened.

2 Mix the eggs and milk together and add to the pan. Using a wooden spoon, stir constantly to ensure the egg doesn't stick. Continue to cook the egg until it is semi-solid and creamy – this should take about 3 minutes.

3 Remove from the heat – the egg will keep warm due to the heat from the pan. Warm the tortilla in the oven, then spoon the scrambled egg on top and roll up. Cut in half horizontally to serve.

Knob of butter

1 teaspoon olive oil

¼ red pepper, deseeded and diced

1 spring onion, finely chopped

2 sun-dried tomatoes in oil, chopped

4 medium free-range eggs, lightly beaten

2 tablespoons milk

Serves 1–2

TOMATO & EGG NAN

Small nan bread are surprisingly versatile and they make an excellent alternative to regular sliced bread. Here, they are topped with a simple tomato sauce and slices of hard-boiled egg.

FOR THE TOMATO SAUCE

1 tablespoon olive oil

1 clove garlic, crushed

200 g passata (sieved tomatoes)

1 tablespoon tomato purée

½ teaspoon paprika

¼ teaspoon sugar or maple syrup

TO SERVE

2 free-range eggs

2 small nan bread

Serves 2 (tomato sauce serves 4)

1 To make the tomato sauce, heat the oil in a heavy-based frying pan. Add the garlic and cook for 1 minute until softened but not browned. Add the passata, tomato purée, paprika and sugar or maple syrup and cook for 10–15 minutes until reduced and thickened.

2 Meanwhile, cook the eggs in plenty of boiling water for about 5 minutes until hard-boiled. Alternatively, you can fry the eggs in a little oil or poach them in water.

3 Warm the nan bread in a toaster or dry frying pan. Serve topped with a few spoonfuls of tomato sauce and slices of the hard-boiled or fried egg.

6 TO 8 MONTHS
Mash the well-cooked hard-boiled egg into a few spoonfuls of the tomato sauce and serve with slices of warm nan.

BABY FALAFEL BURGERS

These tasty burgers are made from chickpeas which are a good source of iron, zinc, folate and vitamin E. Serve in mini bread rolls with slices of cucumber and tomato, and humous, mayonnaise or ketchup.

400 g can chickpeas, drained and rinsed

3 spring onions, chopped

2 cloves garlic, crushed

1 teaspoon ground cumin

1 teaspoon ground coriander

1 egg, beaten

Flour, for dusting

Vegetable oil, for frying

Makes 6 burgers

1 Blend the chickpeas, spring onions, garlic, cumin and coriander in a food processor. Add the egg and blend again until the mixture forms a coarse paste, then place the mixture in the refrigerator for 1 hour.

2 Form the mixture into 6 burgers with floured hands. Roll each burger in flour until lightly coated.

3 Heat 1 tablespoon oil in a large frying pan. Cook the burgers in batches (adding more oil if necessary) for 6 minutes, turning once, until golden.

8 MONTHS TO 1 YEAR
Mash or purée the burgers with tomato sauce or humous.

SPICY BEAN KOFTAS

These lightly spiced red kidney bean balls are delicious served in warm pitta bread with a tahini dressing and a little salad.

1   Heat the olive oil in a heavy-based frying pan and fry the onion for 8 minutes until softened. Add the garlic, cumin, coriander, paprika and kidney beans and cook for a further 5 minutes.

2   Remove from the heat and put the mixture into a bowl. Mash well until it forms a coarse paste and leave to cool. When cool, place in the refrigerator for 30 minutes to allow the mixture to firm.

3   Using floured hands, form the mixture into 16 walnut-sized balls and roll in flour until coated.

4   Heat enough oil to cover the base of a heavy-based frying pan. Fry the balls in batches for 8 minutes, turning occasionally, until golden. Drain on kitchen paper.

5   To make the tahini dressing, combine the tahini, natural yogurt and oil.

6   To serve, warm 4 mini pitta breads and slice them in half. Fill each pitta bread half with 2 kofta balls, a spoonful of tahini dressing and some sliced tomato and shredded lettuce. Serve immediately.

FOR THE KOFTAS

1 tablespoon olive oil

1 medium onion, finely chopped

2 cloves garlic, crushed

1 teaspoon ground cumin

1 teaspoon ground coriander

1 teaspoon paprika

400 g can red kidney beans, drained and rinsed

Flour, for dusting

Vegetable oil, for frying

FOR THE TAHINI DRESSING

1 tablespoon light tahini

3 tablespoons natural yogurt

2 teaspoons extra-virgin olive oil

Makes 16 balls

FILLED JACKET POTATOES

2 x 225 g baking potatoes

1 tablespoon sunflower oil

Serves 2

Wholesome, nutritious and easy to prepare, you can't go wrong with a jacket potato. Here are a few ideas for appetising and healthy fillings.

1 Preheat the oven to 200°C, gas mark 6. Scrub the potatoes and prick them with a fork in several places.

2 Coat the potatoes in oil. Bake them in the centre of the oven for about 1 hour 15 minutes, or until the skins are crisp and cooked through.

3 Remove the potatoes from the oven and cut them in half lengthways. Serve with your choice of the following fillings:

Pesto & Avocado *Mash the flesh of a medium, ripe avocado. Add 1 tablespoon mayonnaise, 1 teaspoon lemon juice and 1 tablespoon vegetarian pesto and mix well. Spoon over the potatoes and sprinkle with vegetarian Parmesan cheese.*

Humous & Roasted Red Pepper *Toss ½ medium red pepper in 1 tablespoon olive oil, and roast for 25–30 minutes, turning occasionally. Cut the pepper into small pieces and combine with 4 tablespoons humous. Spoon over baked potatoes.*

Cream Cheese & Leek *Fry 1 medium sliced leek in 1 tablespoon olive oil for 5 minutes until softened. Remove from the heat and stir in 4 heaped tablespoons cream cheese. Spoon over the potatoes and sprinkle with finely chopped chives.*

SPRING ROLLS WITH SWEET PLUM DIPPING SAUCE

Children will love these bite-sized spring rolls, which are full of crispy noodles and vegetables. They can even help to make them.

1   Soak the noodles in hot water for 3 minutes or as instructed on the packet, then drain and cut into short lengths using scissors.

2   Heat the oils in a wok. Add the carrots, green beans and spring onions and stir-fry for 2 minutes. Add the ginger, beansprouts and soy sauce, then stir-fry over a medium-high heat for 2 minutes, stirring continuously, until the liquid evaporates but the vegetables are still moist. Stir in the noodles, then put the vegetable and noodle mixture into a bowl and leave to cool.

3   Place one spring roll wrapper on a flat surface, keeping the rest of the wrappers covered with a tea towel to prevent them drying out. Place a tablespoon of the filling on the corner nearest you, then fold the corner over the filling towards the centre. Fold in the 2 sides of the wrapper, then continue to roll. Brush the far corner with a little egg white and roll over to seal the parcel. Repeat with the remaining filling and wrappers, making 16 spring rolls altogether.

4   To cook the spring rolls, pour oil into a wok until it is about 1 cm deep. Heat the oil and fry the spring rolls in batches for about 6–8 minutes, turning them until they are crisp and golden. Remove from the wok with a slotted spoon and drain on kitchen paper. Keep the spring rolls warm by covering them in foil while you fry the rest.

5   To make the dipping sauce, combine the plum sauce with the soy sauce in a small bowl. Serve with the spring rolls.

FOR THE SPRING ROLLS

50 g vermicelli rice noodles

1 tablespoon vegetable oil, plus extra for frying

1 teaspoon toasted sesame oil

2 medium carrots, cut into thin strips

150 g green beans, sliced and blanched

2 spring onions, finely sliced

2.5 cm piece of fresh ginger, grated

50 g beansprouts

1 tablespoon soy sauce

16 small spring roll wrappers, 12 cm x 12 cm, defrosted

1 free-range egg white, lightly beaten

FOR THE DIPPING SAUCE

3 tablespoons sweet plum sauce

1 tablespoon soy sauce

Makes 16 rolls

MINI POTATO, CHEESE & ONION PASTIES

175 g potatoes, cut into bite-sized chunks

25 g butter

4 spring onions, finely sliced

70 g canned unsweetened, reduced-salt sweetcorn, drained and rinsed

1 tablespoon fresh parsley, finely chopped

40 g vegetarian Cheddar cheese, grated

375 g ready-rolled puff pastry

1 free-range egg, beaten, to glaze

Makes 10 pasties

These child-friendly-sized pasties can be served warm for lunch or tea, accompanied with new potatoes and vegetables. They also make a great addition to a lunchbox.

1 Preheat the oven to 200°C, gas mark 6. Boil the potatoes in plenty of boiling water for 10–15 minutes until tender. Drain well and leave to cool.

2 Meanwhile, melt the butter in a heavy-based frying pan and cook the spring onions for 2 minutes until softened. Add the spring onions to the potatoes with the sweetcorn, parsley and cheese.

3 Place the pastry on a board or work surface and roll out until about 3 mm thick. Cut into 20 rounds using a 9 cm cutter. Place 1 heaped teaspoon of the potato mixture in the middle of 10 of the pastry circles, leaving a gap around the edge.

4 Brush the edges of each pastry round with beaten egg and place another pastry round on top. Seal the edges using your fingers and crimp with a fork. Brush the top with beaten egg and make an air hole with a fork.

5 Place the pasties on a baking sheet and bake for 15-20 minutes until risen and golden.

Soya Mince & Vegetable Pasties Cover 25 g dried soya mince with water. Add ½ teaspoon yeast extract and stir until dissolved. Leave the soya for 15 minutes, until it is rehydrated. Meanwhile, steam 1 small diced potato and 1 small diced carrot until tender. Heat 1 teaspoon of vegetable oil in a pan and sauté 1 small chopped onion for 5 minutes. Add 1 crushed clove of garlic and sauté for a further 2 minutes until the onion has softened. Add the carrot, potato, 1 tablespoon finely chopped fresh parsley, the mince, 2 tablespoons passata and 1 tablespoon of soy sauce. Mix well and cook for 10 minutes. Using this filling, make the pasties following the method above.

6 TO 8 MONTHS
The pasty filling is suitable for babies, but mash or purée before serving.

HUMOUS

400 g can chickpeas, drained and rinsed

1–2 cloves garlic, crushed

2 tablespoons light tahini

Juice of 1 lemon

4 tablespoons olive oil

Paprika, for sprinkling (optional)

Serves 10

This humous can be kept for up to 5 days if stored in an airtight container in the refrigerator.

1 Place the chickpeas and garlic in a food processor or blender and blend to a coarse paste. Add the tahini and the lemon juice and blend until smooth.

2 While the food processor is running, gradually add the oil. Spoon the humous into a bowl and drizzle with more olive oil. For added colour you can sprinkle the humous with paprika.

The recipes on this page are great for kids – they make quick and easy snacks, which are also nutritious. They can be used as sandwich fillings, spread onto toast or served with dunkers. Fresh, crisp vegetables make great healthy dunkers – carrot, celery, cucmber and pepper, cut into sticks, work well, particularly as they are brightly coloured. Other options include crisps, nachos, breadsticks, tortillas, corn chips and poppadums or nan bread, broken into pieces or cut into fingers.

Bean Dip

The garlic in this tangy creamy dip is roasted to give it a more mellow flavour.

1. Preheat the oven to 180°C, gas mark 4. Place the garlic on a baking tray and roast for 30 minutes until soft. Peel off the skin.

2. Place the beans, garlic, lemon juice, mint and olive oil in a food processor or blender and process until smooth.

4 cloves garlic, left whole in their skins

400 g can cannellini beans, drained and rinsed

Juice of 1 lemon

1 tablespoon mint leaves, freshly chopped

2 tablespoons olive oil

Serves 10

Guacamole

The creamy texture and bright colour of this Mexican-style dip really appeals to children.

Scoop out the flesh of the avocado, place in a bowl, then mash until smooth. Add the lemon juice, tomato, mayonnaise and garlic. Mix well until combined. Store in the refrigerator before serving to prevent the avocado from discolouring.

1 large avocado

1 tablespoon lemon juice

2 medium tomatoes, deseeded and chopped

1 tablespoon mayonnaise

1 small clove garlic, crushed

Serves 4

Three Nut Butter

By making your own nut butter, you can ensure it contains only the ingredients you want and no additives, unwanted fat or sugar. You can use whatever combination of nuts you like.

1. Toast the nuts in a dry frying pan for a couple of minutes. Transfer the nuts to a food processor or blender and process until finely ground.

2. Pour the oil into the blender or food processor and blend the mixture to a coarse paste. Store in an airtight jar or container in the refrigerator for up to a week.

25 g unsalted almonds, shelled

25 g unsalted cashew nuts

25 g unsalted peanuts, shelled

3–4 tablespoons sunflower oil

Makes 10 portions

HOMEMADE BAKED BEANS

1 tablespoon olive oil

200 g can low-sugar and salt haricot beans, drained and rinsed

150 ml passata (sieved tomatoes)

1–2 teaspoons Dijon mustard

1 tablespoon vegetarian Worcestershire sauce

1 tablespoon maple syrup

1 tablespoon tomato purée

Serves 2

Making your own baked beans is really very simple. They are a healthy alternative to commercially produced beans, which often contain excessive amounts of sugar and salt. Do not give baked beans to young babies in large quanities as they are high in fibre and can be difficult to digest.

1   Place all the ingredients in a heavy-based saucepan and mix together. Bring to the boil, then reduce the heat and simmer for 10 minutes.

2   Half-cover the pan and simmer for a further 10 minutes until the beans are tender and the sauce has reduced and thickened.

SESAME POTATO WEDGES WITH GARLIC DIP

FOR THE POTATO WEDGES

675 g potatoes, scrubbed and cut into wedges

1–2 tablespoons olive oil

1 teaspoon sesame seeds

FOR THE GARLIC DIP

1–2 cloves garlic, left whole in their skin

6 tablespoons mayonnaise

Serves 4

These potato wedges retain their nutritious skin and are baked in the oven, which keeps fat levels down. If your little one does not like garlic, simply serve them with mayonnaise, humous or ketchup.

1   Preheat the oven to 200°C, gas mark 6. Toss the potatoes and garlic in the oil and place on a baking tray. Bake for 15 minutes, then remove from the oven. Turn the potatoes, making sure they are thoroughly coated in the oil, and sprinkle with the sesame seeds.

2   Return the potatoes and garlic to the oven for a further 15–20 minutes until tender and golden.

3   To make the garlic dip, remove the roasted garlic from the potatoes, peel and mash with a fork. Combine the garlic with the mayonnaise in a bowl and serve with the potato wedges.

Sweet Potato Wedges *For more unusual potato wedges, use sweet potatoes. The orange fleshed variety are tasty and are rich in vitamin C and beta carotene.*

8 MONTHS TO 1 YEAR
These potato wedges make great finger food for your baby.

HONEYED CORN ON THE COB

Glossy and sweet, this corn-on-the-cob is fun and messy to eat – serve with napkins or kitchen paper!

1   Cook the corn in boiling water for 5 minutes until tender. Drain well.

2   Heat the butter in a heavy-based saucepan until melted. Mix in the honey, then add the corn to the pan. Make sure the corn is coated thoroughly in the honey mixture and cook for 4 minutes until golden.

1 corn on the cob, halved

15 g butter

1 teaspoon honey

Serves 2

CRUNCHY APPLE COLESLAW

2 tablespoons extra-virgin olive oil

1 tablespoon white wine vinegar

4 tablespoons mayonnaise

115 g white cabbage, finely shredded

1 medium carrot, grated

1–2 spring onions, finely sliced

1 dessert apple, cored and diced

2 tablespoons sunflower or pumpkin seeds, toasted and chopped

Serves 4–6

Commercially made coleslaw often contains unwanted additives, but it only takes a matter of minutes to make your own, healthier version.

1   To make the dressing, whisk together the olive oil, vinegar and mayonnaise in a small bowl.

2   Place the cabbage, carrot, spring onions and apple in a salad bowl and mix together well. Spoon over the dressing and toss to coat the salad. Stir in the sunflower or pumpkin seeds before serving.

COUNTRY GARDEN SALAD

1 tablespoon extra-virgin olive oil

1 teaspoon white wine vinegar

1 teaspoon mayonnaise

8 cherry tomatoes, halved

4 baby corn, blanched and sliced into rounds

8 white or black seedless grapes, halved

3 slices green pepper

2 vegetarian cheese slices

Serves 2

Encourage your child to eat salad by cutting the green pepper and cheese into geometric shapes. Feel free to change the ingredients in this salad – carrots, red pepper, cucumber, watercress or toasted chopped nuts and seeds all make delicious additions.

1   To make the dressing, whisk together the oil, vinegar and mayonnaise.

2   Place the tomatoes, corn and grapes in a bowl. Spoon over the dressing and toss well.

3   Cut the green pepper and cheese slices into small pieces and sprinkle over the top of the salad.

8 MONTHS TO 1 YEAR
The individual fruit, vegetables and cheese can be given to babies from 8 months as finger food.

Packed Lunches

It can be a challenge to provide interesting and varied packed lunches for children that won't take ages to prepare and that they will enjoy. This chapter contains tempting ideas that will withstand the journey to school.

SECRET ROLLS

1 crunchy bread roll

Butter, for spreading

2 tablespoons vegetarian pesto
(see recipe page 60)

1 vegetarian cheese slice, halved

Handful fresh spinach leaves

Serves 1

Kids love this inventive lunchtime snack – the stripy filling is only revealed when they bite into the roll.

1 Slice off the top of the roll and scoop out most of the centre. Butter the inside of the roll, including the 'lid'.

2 Spread a layer of pesto in the roll, then top with a double layer of cheese. Arrange a few spinach leaves on top of the cheese, then spread with another layer of pesto.

3 Replace the 'lid' and wrap the roll in cling film. Press down lightly and refrigerate overnight to allow the flavours to mingle.

Humous & Salad Secret Rolls *Replace the cheese and pesto with humous and slices of cucumber and diced tomato.*

DOUBLE DECKERS

2 slices wholemeal bread

1 slice white bread

Butter

Cream cheese

Yeast extract

Serves 1

Arrange slices of white and wholemeal bread, or other varieties of bread, on top of one another for this triple-layered sandwich.

Spread the bread with butter. Spread a slice of wholemeal bread with cream cheese and top with a slice of white bread. Spread the white bread with yeast extract and top with a second piece of wholemeal. Cut the sandwich into triangles.

Pinwheel Sandwiches *For a pinwheel effect, make the sandwich, remove the crusts and roll the sandwich up. Wrap in clingfilm and refrigerate overnight. The next morning, slice the sandwich into rounds.*

PITTA POCKETS

Kids can get bored of sandwiches, so try these mini pitta breads which make an interesting alternative to sliced bread or rolls.

Slice the pitta bread lengthways, then spoon some coleslaw inside. Tuck in slices of falafel, then press down the top of the bread.

Guacamole & Alfafa Pitta Pockets *Replace the coleslaw with guacamole (see recipe page 35) and alfalfa sprouts for a creamy and crunchy filling.*

1–2 mini pitta breads

Coleslaw (see recipe page 38)

Falafel, cooked and sliced horizontally

Serves 1

FRITTATA CIABATTA

This Italian-style omelette contains a healthy selection of vegetables. It can be made the night before serving and will keep for up to 2 days in the fridge. It is tasty served cold for lunch, or warm for an evening snack.

1   Boil the potatoes for 10 minutes, or until tender, then drain well. Meanwhile, fry the spring onions in the oil and butter in a large frying pan for 2 minutes, then add the peas. Cook, stirring, for 1 minute, then remove from the pan.

2   Arrange the potatoes in the bottom of the pan, then top with the cooked vegetables. Pour the eggs over the vegetables, then sprinkle with cheese and arrange the sliced tomato on top. Cook over a moderate heat for 5–6 minutes until the eggs are set.

3   Place the pan under a preheated grill and cook the top of the frittata for about 3 minutes until set and golden. Cut into wedges and serve in a chunk of ciabatta with tomato ketchup.

3 medium potatoes, thinly sliced

2 spring onions, finely chopped

½ tablespoon olive oil

Small knob butter

55 g frozen peas

6 medium free-range eggs, beaten

85 g vegetarian Cheddar cheese, grated

1 medium tomato, sliced

Ciabatta bread, to serve

Tomato ketchup, to serve

Serves 6

SPINACH & MOZZARELLA CALZONE

These cute little folded pizzas are delicious served cold and make a change from sandwiches or rolls.

FOR THE DOUGH

1 teaspoon dried yeast

250 g Italian OO flour or strong white bread flour, plus extra for dusting

1 teaspoon salt

¼ teaspoon sugar

1 tablespoon olive oil, plus extra for greasing

180 ml lukewarm water

FOR THE FILLING

1 tablespoon olive oil

1 large clove garlic, finely chopped

1 teaspoon dried oregano

300 ml passata (sieved tomatoes)

Pinch of sugar

175 g fresh spinach, rinsed

40 g vegetarian Cheddar cheese, grated

150 g vegetarian mozzarella, torn into small pieces

Makes 8

1   To make the dough, mix together the yeast, flour, salt and sugar in a large bowl. Make a well in the centre and add the oil and water. Gradually draw the dry ingredients into the water and oil using a palette knife and then your hands to form a ball of dough.

2   On a lightly floured work surface, knead the dough for 15 minutes until it is smooth and elastic. Put the dough in a lightly oiled bowl, cover with clingfilm and put in a warm place for 1 hour until it has doubled in size.

3   Meanwhile, make the filling. Heat the oil in a heavy-based frying pan and fry the garlic for 1 minute until softened. Add the oregano, passata and sugar and cook for 15 minutes until reduced and thickened.

4   Preheat the oven to 220°C, gas mark 7. Steam the spinach over a little water for about 2 minutes, until wilted. Drain well and squeeze out any excess water with your hands, then chop roughly. Mix the spinach into the tomato sauce.

5   Knock back the dough using your knuckles, then divide into 8 pieces. Roll each piece into a thin round, about 12 cm in diameter. Spoon a heaped tablespoon of the tomato and spinach sauce into the centre of one circle, then top with a sprinkling of Cheddar cheese and mozzarella. Brush the edge of the dough with water, then fold in half to make a semi-circle shape. Firmly press the edges together and crimp to seal. Prick the top with a fork, then repeat to make 8 parcels.

6   Place the calzone on a lightly greased large baking sheet and bake for 10–12 minutes until golden.

6 TO 8 MONTHS

The tomato and spinach sauce can be given to babies from 6 months. Purée or chop depending on the age of your baby and sprinkle with cheese, if liked. The sauce can be mixed with pasta or rice.

BEAN & PASTA SOUP

Many lunchboxes now come with a resilient flask, but you can also buy small ones separately to keep soup warm for lunch time. This hearty soup is ideal for warming up small tummies on a cold winter's day.

1 tablespoon olive oil

1 small onion, finely chopped

1 small carrot, finely chopped

1 small stick celery, finely chopped

50 ml canned chopped tomatoes

1 teaspoon dried oregano

450 ml vegetable stock

140 g canned cannellini beans, drained

40 g small soup pasta

Serves 2

1 Heat the oil in a large saucepan and fry the onion for 8 minutes, until softened. Add the carrot and celery and cook, covered, for 5 minutes, stirring frequently.

2 Add the tomatoes, oregano and vegetable stock and bring to the boil. Reduce the heat and simmer, half covered, for 15–20 minutes until the stock has reduced and the vegetables are tender.

3 Add the beans and pasta and cook for about 10 minutes, or until the pasta is just tender.

MELON & FETA SALAD

Fruit and soft cheese are a refreshing combination in this summer salad. It keeps well if made the night before.

1 wedge melon, preferably Charentais or Cantaloupe

40 g vegetarian feta cheese, cubed

Squeeze of fresh lemon juice

½ tablespoon olive oil

Serves 1

Place the melon and feta in a container with a lid. Add the lemon juice and oil, seal the container and turn to coat the melon and feta in the dressing. Refrigerate until ready to take to school.

MOZZARELLA & TOMATO SALAD

Kids love the texture and taste of the mozzarella in this classic salad.

1 teaspoon balsamic vinegar

1 teaspoon olive oil

40 g vegetarian mozzarella, cubed

5 cherry tomatoes, halved

Serves 1

1 To make the dressing, mix together the balsamic vinegar and olive oil.

2 Place the mozzarella and cherry tomatoes in a container with a lid. Drizzle with the dressing and refrigerate until ready to take to school.

SUMMER PASTA SALAD

This light pasta salad is quick and easy to prepare. It can be made the night before, but add the tomatoes the following morning. Store in an airtight container.

1 Cook the pasta following the manufacturer's instructions until *al dente*, then drain well.

2 Add the pepper, sweetcorn, tomato, mayonnaise and pesto to the pasta and mix well until combined.

50 g fusilli pasta

¼ small red pepper, deseeded and diced

3 tablespoons canned sweetcorn, drained

1 small tomato, deseeded and diced

1 tablespoon mayonnaise

1 teaspoon vegetarian red pesto

Serves 1

VEGETABLE CRISPS

Ready-made crisps, especially flavoured ones, are often laden with additives, flavourings (some of which are not vegetarian) and the dreadful monosodium glutamate. Although making your own may seem a bit of an effort, they are incredibly easy and will keep for a few days if kept in an airtight container.

1 Thinly slice the potato, carrot, beetroot and parsnip in a food processor.

2 Pour the oil into a wok until it is about 6 cm deep (you can use a deep-fat fryer, if you have one). Heat the oil until it reaches smoking point.

3 Fry a few of the vegetable slices at a time, until they are golden – each batch will take about 2–3 minutes. Drain well on kitchen paper and repeat until all the crisps are cooked.

1 large potato

1 medium carrot

1 medium raw beetroot

1 medium parsnip

Sunflower or groundnut oil, for frying

Serves 4

VEGETABLE STICKS WITH SATAY DIP

Kids find vegetables more appealing when they are accompanied by a dip. Choose any fresh vegetables you like to dunk into this creamy peanut sauce.

2 tablespoons smooth peanut butter

1 teaspoon olive oil

1 teaspoon hot water

1 teaspoon soy sauce

½ teaspoon soft light brown sugar

2 tablespoons mayonnaise

Cucumber, pepper, celery, carrot and mangetout, cut into sticks

Serves 2

To make the dip, combine all the ingredients in a small bowl and mix well. Spoon into a bowl and serve with the vegetable sticks.

VEGETABLE & LENTIL PATE

This delicious and simple pâté is great on crackers or in a crunchy bread roll.

1 tablespoon olive oil

1 medium onion, finely chopped

1 large clove garlic, crushed

1 stick of celery, finely chopped

1 teaspoon dried mixed herbs

1 medium carrot, grated

85 g red lentils, rinsed

250 ml water

1 teaspoon bouillon powder

Serves 8–10

1   Heat the oil in a heavy-based frying pan. Fry the onion for 8 minutes until softened. Add the garlic and celery and fry for 5 minutes, stirring occasionally. Add the herbs and carrot and cook, stirring, for another 5 minutes.

2   Meanwhile, place the lentils in a saucepan with the water. Add the bouillon powder and cook for 15–20 minutes until the lentils are tender and mushy. Drain, if necessary, and combine with the onion mixture. If the pâté is too coarse for your liking, blend in a food processor until smooth.

8 MONTHS TO 1 YEAR
This pâté is suitable for babies from 8 months, but leave out the bouillon powder and purée or mash.

MINI QUICHES

These are just the right size for small hands to handle and they hold together well in a lunch box. Here, puff pastry is used but you could use shortcrust pastry, if preferred.

1 Preheat the oven to 200°C, gas mark 6. Grease a deep 6-hole muffin tin. Roll out the puff pastry until it is quite thin and press it into the 6 muffin holes. Trim the tops and chill for 30 minutes.

2 Combine the eggs, milk and cheese, reserving a little cheese for sprinkling. Pour the mixture into the muffin tin. Top each pie with a slice of tomato and sprinkle with the reserved cheese.

3 Bake for 20–25 minutes until risen and golden. Leave to cool slightly before removing the pies from the tin.

Butter, for greasing

200 g ready-rolled puff pastry

3 medium free-range eggs, beaten

125 ml milk

55 g vegetarian Cheddar cheese, grated

1 medium tomato, sliced

Makes 6

SPAGHETTI OMELETTE

This is a great addition to a lunchbox and keeps well if made in advance. It's also a good way of using up any leftover pasta. Serve cut into wedges with cherry tomatoes.

75 g spaghetti

Olive oil, for coating

15 g butter

3 medium free-range eggs, beaten

60 g vegetarian Parmesan cheese, grated

Serves 4

1 Cook the spaghetti in plenty of boiling water, following the manufacturer's instructions. Drain well and toss in a little oil, then leave to cool.

2 Melt the butter in a medium-sized frying pan, then arrange the pasta in the bottom of the pan.

3 Mix together the eggs and Parmesan cheese and pour the mixture over the pasta. Cook for 5 minutes, or until the base is set and golden, then brown the top under a preheated grill. Cut into wedges before serving.

Vegetable Omelette Add chopped sweet pepper, spring onion or tomato to the egg mixture.

APPLE FLAPJACKS

These wholesome, sustaining oaty biscuits make a popular lunchtime treat.

120 g butter

3 tablespoons golden syrup

150 g soft brown sugar

240 g porridge oats

30 g sunflower seeds

1 medium dessert apple, cored and grated

Pinch of salt

Makes 16 flapjacks

1 Preheat the oven to 175°C, gas mark 4. Grease and line a 20 cm × 20 cm cake tin.

2 Heat the butter, golden syrup and sugar in a saucepan until melted, then stir until combined.

3 Remove from the heat and stir in the oats, sunflower seeds, apple and salt, then pour the mixture into the prepared cake tin.

4 Bake for 20–25 minutes, until slightly crisp and golden. Leave to cool for 5 minutes, then turn out onto a wire rack. Cut the flapjack into squares while still warm.

SANDWICH FILLERS

Early mornings are not usually conducive to creativity and it's a challenge to provide interesting and varied sandwiches every day. Time is also at a premium and so most of the following ideas can be prepared the night before. Try varying the choice of bread you use, from ciabatta and bagels to nan and mini rolls. Pastry cutters are also a great way of making different shaped sandwiches and adding extra interest.

- Bagel with chopped hard-boiled egg, vegetarian bacon and sliced tomato
- Tortilla with mozzarella, pesto and tomato
- Cottage cheese and finely chopped pineapple
- Vegetarian sausage with sliced tomato, alfalfa and mayonnaise
- Vegetable and lentil pâté (see recipe page 48) with cucumber in a mini nan
- Humous (see recipe page 34) and grated carrot
- Roasted vegetables with humous
- Sliced hard-boiled egg, spring onion and mayonnaise in a rolled tortilla
- Grated apple and cheese in a soft wholemeal bap
- Mashed avocado, chopped tomato and falafel
- Muffin with cream cheese and yeast extract
- Bean pâté and lettuce
- Ciabatta with olive pâté and tomato
- Three nut butter (see recipe page 35) with banana or strawberry jam

LUNCHBOX SNACKS

It can be tempting to resort to quick and easy lunchbox fillers, such as packets of crisps and chocolate biscuits, so here are some ideas for more nutritious alternatives.

- Cherry tomatoes
- Vegetable sticks with guacamole
- Breadsticks with cream cheese dip
- Scone with cream cheese and strawberry jam
- Rice cakes sandwiched with chocolate spread and sliced banana
- Malt loaf or fruit bread
- Small box of raisins
- Pot of fromage frais
- Nuts and raisins
- Toasted mixed sunflower, pumpkin and sesame seeds

4 Main Meals

The recipes in this chapter will appeal to adults and children alike, saving the need to prepare separate meals for the kids and making it easy for the family to eat together.

MOUSSAKA

The small chunks of peeled aubergine in this recipe are more child-friendly than the large slices found in traditional moussaka. Serve with a salad and garlic bread.

I medium aubergine, peeled and diced

Salt, for sprinkling aubergine

2 tablespoons olive oil

I medium onion, diced

I clove garlic, chopped

I red pepper, cored, deseeded and diced

I teaspoon dried oregano

I medium courgette, finely chopped

85 g mushrooms, finely chopped

225 g vegetarian mince

400 g can chopped tomatoes

I tablespoon tomato purée

400 g natural yogurt

2 free-range eggs, beaten

25 g vegetarian Parmesan cheese, grated

25 g vegetarian Cheddar cheese, grated

Serves 4

1 Preheat the oven to 200°C, gas mark 6. Arrange the diced aubergine in an even layer on a plate and sprinkle liberally with salt. Leave for an hour to release any bitter juices, then rinse well and pat dry with kitchen paper.

2 Heat the oil in a large, heavy-based saucepan. Add the onion and fry for 8 minutes over a low heat until softened. Add the garlic, pepper, oregano, courgette, mushrooms and aubergine. Cover and cook for 10 minutes stirring occasionally, until the vegetables are tender.

3 Add the vegetarian mince, tomatoes and tomato purée. Cook, half-covered, for 10 minutes until the sauce has reduced and thickened – if it seems too dry, add a little vegetable stock or water. Spoon the mixture into an ovenproof dish.

4 To make the topping, beat together the yogurt and eggs. Spoon this mixture over the vegetables and level with the back of a spoon. Sprinkle with both cheeses and bake for 25 minutes until golden.

Traditional Moussaka *To make a moussaka with layers of aubergine, in the traditional way, fry slices of aubergine separately from the other vegetables. Arrange the vegetable mixture in the dish and top with a layer of aubergine, then more vegetables and a final layer of aubergine. Spoon the yogurt and egg mixture over the aubergine and sprinkle with both cheeses before baking.*

6 TO 8 MONTHS

This recipe is suitable for babies over 6 months. Mash or purée, depending on the age of your baby.

VEGETABLE HOT POT

Most children love garlic bread and it makes a great topping for this vegetable and bean casserole. This complete meal in one pot needs little else, although a green salad would make a good accompaniment.

1 Preheat the oven to 200°C, gas mark 6. Arrange the diced aubergine in an even layer on a plate and sprinkle liberally with salt. Leave for an hour to release any bitter juices, then rinse well and pat dry with kitchen paper.

2 Heat 1 tablespoon of the oil and fry the aubergine for 8 minutes until golden, then remove from the pan and set aside. Add the remaining oil to the pan and fry the onion for 5 minutes, until softened. Add the garlic, courgette, mushrooms, red pepper, mixed herbs and oregano and cook for 10 minutes over a medium heat until the vegetables are tender.

3 Add the tomatoes, tomato chutney, beans, chilli powder (if using) and cooked aubergine and cook for 15 minutes until the sauce has reduced and thickened. Spoon the mixture into an ovenproof casserole dish.

4 Rub the garlic over the baguette slices and arrange in a layer on top of the vegetable and bean mixture. Brush liberally with oil and sprinkle the cheese over the top. Bake for 20 minutes until golden.

FOR THE HOT POT

1 medium aubergine, peeled and diced

Salt, for sprinkling aubergine

3 tablespoons olive oil

1 medium onion, finely chopped

2 cloves garlic, finely chopped

1 medium courgette, diced

2 large, flat mushrooms, finely chopped

1 red pepper, cored, deseeded and sliced

1 teaspoon mixed dried herbs

1 teaspoon dried oregano

400 g can chopped tomatoes

1 tablespoon tomato chutney

400 g can mixed beans, rinsed and drained

1 teaspoon mild chilli powder (optional)

FOR THE TOPPING

1 small baguette, sliced into 1 cm rounds

1 clove garlic, halved

Olive oil, for brushing

55 g vegetarian Cheddar cheese, grated

Serves 4

HEARTY GOULASH WITH HERBY DUMPLINGS

A winter warmer that can be made in advance and reheated in the oven when required. Serve with green vegetables for a wholesome meal.

FOR THE GOULASH

1 tablespoon olive oil

1 medium onion, chopped

1 clove garlic, finely chopped

1 small red pepper, cored, deseeded and diced

175 g butternut squash, cubed

350 g potatoes, cubed

1 teaspoon caraway seeds

1 tablespoon paprika

1 tablespoon plain flour

400 g can chopped tomatoes

300 ml vegetable stock

150 ml soured cream

FOR THE DUMPLINGS

40 g vegetable suet

85 g self-raising flour

½ teaspoon salt

1 tablespoon fresh sage, chopped

1 tablespoon fresh rosemary, chopped

5 tablespoons water

Serves 4

1   Preheat the oven to 180°C, gas mark 4. Heat the oil in a large, heavy-based pan. Add the onion and fry for 8 minutes until softened. Add the garlic, red pepper, squash, potatoes and caraway seeds and cook, half-covered, for a further 10 minutes, stirring occasionally.

2   Stir in the paprika and flour and cook for 1 minute, then add the tomatoes and stock. Bring to the boil, then reduce the heat and simmer, half-covered, for 20 minutes, stirring occasionally, until the vegetables soften and the sauce starts to reduce and thicken. Transfer to a casserole dish with a lid.

3   Meanwhile, make the dumplings. Place the suet, flour, salt, sage and rosemary in a large bowl. Gradually add the water, mixing with a fork and then your hands, to make a soft, sticky dough. Using floured hands, form the dough into 8 dumplings and arrange on top of the goulash.

4   Place the goulash in the oven and cook, covered, for 20 minutes. Cook uncovered for a further 10 minutes until the dumplings have risen. Remove the casserole from the oven and remove the dumplings. Stir the soured cream into the goulash and serve accompanied by the dumplings.

6 TO 8 MONTHS

If cooking for your baby, use water instead of stock, as stock is high in salt. Purée or mash the goulash, including the dumplings, depending on the age of your baby.

WINTER BAKE

This delicious pie is just the thing for a cold winter's night. The bright colours will appeal to children – vibrant orange layers of sweet potato contrast with a bright green layer of leeks, spinach and peas.

1. Preheat the oven to 200°C, gas mark 6. Cook the potatoes and sweet potatoes in plenty of boiling water for 15–20 minutes until tender.

2. Heat the oil in a heavy-based frying pan and fry the leek for 5 minutes until softened. Add the oregano or thyme and the spinach (if using) and cook for 3 minutes. Stir in the petit pois and remove from the heat.

3. Drain the potatoes and add the butter, milk, cream (if using) and mustard. Mash the potatoes until smooth and creamy. Butter an ovenproof dish and spoon half of the mash into the dish. Smooth with the back of a spoon and top with the leek mixture. Spoon the rest of the mash over the top of the leeks and sprinkle with Cheddar cheese. Bake for 20 minutes until golden.

675 g potatoes, peeled and diced

350 g sweet potatoes, peeled and diced (use the orange-flesh variety)

2 tablespoons olive oil

1 large leek, finely chopped

1 tablespoon dried oregano or thyme

140 g spinach, stalks removed and chopped (optional)

115 g frozen petit pois

55 g butter

150 ml milk, warm

2 tablespoons double cream (optional)

1 tablespoon Dijon mustard

85 g vegetarian Cheddar cheese, grated, plus extra for sprinkling

Serves 4

◆◆◆◆◆◆◆◆◆◆◆◆◆◆

6 TO 8 MONTHS

Reserve a portion of the leek mixture for your baby and combine with a portion of mashed potato. Add a little grated Cheddar cheese and mash until you have the desired consistency. There is no need to bake this mixture.

STAR CASSEROLE

Vegetable casseroles are perfect comfort food, especially this one which is accompanied by golden polenta stars. This dish is warming, sustaining and packed with goodness.

1　To make the polenta stars, bring the water to the boil in a large saucepan and add the salt. Remove the pan from the heat. Gradually pour in the polenta, whisking continuously. Return the pan to the heat and stir constantly for 15 minutes until the polenta is thick and comes away from the side of the pan when stirred. Remove the pan from the heat and stir in the butter, Parmesan cheese and oregano.

2　Spoon the polenta onto a lightly oiled baking sheet. Using a wet spatula, spread it out until it is about 1 cm thick. Leave to cool, then cut into star shapes and set aside.

3　Preheat the grill to high and line the grill pan with foil. Grill the sausages until cooked, then set aside.

4　Meanwhile, heat 2 tablespoons of oil in a heavy-based saucepan. Add the garlic, celery and red pepper and fry for 5 minutes over a medium heat, stirring occasionally, until tender – do not allow the garlic to burn. Add the thyme, mixed herbs and squash and cook for a further 5 minutes.

5　Increase the heat, add the apple juice and boil for 4 minutes. Reduce the heat, add the stock, then simmer for 15–20 minutes until the liquid has reduced and the squash is tender.

6　Meanwhile, place the toasted pine nuts, bread and milk in a blender or food processor and blend until smooth.

7　Slice the sausages and add to the casserole. Then add the pine nut mixture. Heat through, stirring, until it is thickened and creamy.

8　While the casserole is heating through, heat 1 tablespoon of oil in a heavy-based frying pan. Cook the stars in batches for about 3 minutes on each side until golden, using more oil if necessary. Drain on kitchen paper.

9　To serve, spoon the casserole into bowls and surround with polenta stars.

FOR THE POLENTA STARS

800 ml water

1 teaspoon salt

200 g instant polenta

50 g butter

50 g vegetarian Parmesan cheese, grated

1 tablespoon dried oregano

FOR THE CASSEROLE

6 vegetarian sausages

3 tablespoons olive oil, plus extra for greasing

1 large clove garlic, chopped

1 medium stick celery, finely chopped

1 small red pepper, cored, deseeded and chopped

1 teaspoon dried thyme

1 teaspoon dried mixed herbs

550 g butternut squash, peeled, deseeded and cut into bite-sized cubes

300 ml apple juice

350 ml vegetable stock

20 g pine nuts, toasted

1 small slice white bread, crusts removed and cubed

85 ml milk

Serves 4

6 TO 8 MONTHS

Use water instead of stock to reduce the salt content and purée or mash the casserole. Stir a tablespoon of the smooth polenta into your baby's portion.

FRESH PESTO
& PEA PASTA

It's a good idea to familiarise babies and young children with strong flavours and pesto is ideal for this. It's also incredibly versatile – add a spoonful to mashed potato or rice for a quick and simple dish.

FOR THE PESTO

100 g fresh basil leaves, stalks removed

3 cloves garlic, crushed

55 g pine nuts

175 ml olive oil

70 g vegetarian Parmesan cheese, grated

FOR THE PASTA

300 g pasta

75 g frozen petits pois

400 g baby new potatoes, halved

Olive oil, for drizzling

Vegetarian Parmesan cheese, grated, to serve

40 g pine nuts, toasted, to serve

Serves 4

1 To make the pesto, place the basil, garlic and pine nuts in a food processor and process until finely chopped. Gradually add the olive oil, then the Parmesan cheese and blend to a coarse purée. This recipe makes double the quantity of pesto needed – it can be stored in the refrigerator for up to a week.

2 Cook the pasta following the manufacturer's instructions. Add the petits pois 2 minutes before the end of the cooking time. Drain, but leave 3 tablespoons of the cooking water in the pan. Return the pasta and petits pois to the saucepan.

3 Meanwhile, boil the potatoes for 10 minutes, or until tender. Drain and allow to cool slightly before cutting into bite-sized pieces.

4 Add the potatoes to the peas and pasta, and stir in half the pesto. Add a little extra olive oil if the sauce appears dry. Stir well, but gently, until the peas and pasta are thoroughly coated, then heat through.

5 Serve sprinkled with Parmesan cheese and toasted pine nuts.

CREAMY BROCCOLI PASTA BAKE

It can be a real struggle to get children to eat their greens, but cutting them small and immersing them in a creamy cheese sauce makes them more appealing. You can swap the broccoli and cauliflower for peas, carrots, leeks or green beans, if preferred.

1 Cook the pasta in plenty of boiling water according to the manufacturer's instructions. Add the broccoli and cauliflower to the pasta 5 minutes before the end of the cooking time. Drain the pasta and vegetables well and transfer to an ovenproof dish.

2 Meanwhile, make the cheese sauce. Melt the butter in a heavy-based saucepan. Stir in the flour and cook for about 2 minutes, stirring continuously, until the mixture forms a thick paste. Gradually add the warm milk a little at a time, whisking well with a balloon whisk after each addition. Continue to add the milk to make a smooth, creamy sauce.

3 Return the white sauce to the heat and add the mustard and cream cheese (if using). Cook for about 10 minutes until the sauce has thickened. Mix in the Cheddar cheese and stir well until it has melted. Pour the sauce over the pasta and vegetables in the dish and mix gently until combined.

4 Sprinkle with more Cheddar cheese and the breadcrumbs. Grill for 5–10 minutes until the cheese is bubbling and the breadcrumbs are golden.

175 g penne pasta

175 g broccoli, cut into small florets

85 g cauliflower, cut into small florets

25 g butter

3 tablespoons plain flour

700 ml milk, warm

1 tablespoon vegetarian Dijon mustard

2 tablespoons soft cream cheese (optional)

115 g mature vegetarian Cheddar cheese, grated, plus extra for sprinkling

2 tablespoons fresh breadcrumbs

Serves 4

6 TO 8 MONTHS

Purée your baby's portion of the broccoli, pasta and cheese before grilling.

TOMATO & CHICKPEA PASTA

250 g pasta bows

2 tablespoons olive oil

1 large clove garlic, finely chopped

1 teaspoon dried oregano

600 g passata (sieved tomatoes)

1 tablespoon tomato purée

½ teaspoon sugar

200 g can chickpeas, rinsed and drained

2 tablespoons soft cream cheese

Vegetarian Parmesan cheese, freshly grated, to serve

Fresh parsley, finely chopped, to garnish

Serves 4

This pasta makes a nutritious supper dish and only takes a matter of minutes to make. Serve it with steamed broccoli or green beans.

1   Cook the pasta following the manufacturer's instructions. Drain well.

2   Meanwhile, heat the oil in a large, heavy-based saucepan. Add the garlic and oregano and cook over a low-medium heat for 1 minute until softened.

3   Reduce the heat and add the passata, tomato purée, sugar and chickpeas. Cook the sauce for 15 minutes until reduced and thickened. Stir in the cream cheese and heat through.

4   Combine the sauce and pasta and serve in large bowls, sprinkled with Parmesan cheese and parsley.

RAINBOW STIR-FRY WITH NOODLES

250 g vegetarian noodles

1 tablespoon vegetable or groundnut oil

1 teaspoon toasted sesame oil

8 broccoli florets

1 medium carrot, finely shredded

1 small red pepper, deseeded and diced

55 g fine green beans

1 clove garlic, finely chopped

2.5 cm piece fresh ginger, grated

2 teaspoons soy sauce

4 tablespoons apple juice

Spring onions, finely shredded, to garnish

Sesame seeds, to garnish (optional)

Serves 4

Stir-frying is a healthy method of cooking because the vegetables are cooked quickly, ensuring that most nutrients are retained.

1   Cook the noodles in plenty of boiling water, according to the manufacturer's instructions. When just tender, drain well.

2   Meanwhile, heat a wok or a large, heavy-based frying pan. Add the oils, broccoli, carrot, red pepper and beans, and stir-fry for 4 minutes, stirring continuously. Add the garlic and ginger and cook for 1 minute.

3   Pour the soy sauce and apple juice over the vegetables and stir-fry for 2–3 minutes until the vegetables are just tender – add a little water if the stir-fry appears too dry. Serve with the noodles, garnished with the spring onions and sesame seeds (if using).

◆◆◆◆◆◆◆◆ ★ ◆◆◆◆◆◆◆◆

6 TO 8 MONTHS

Purée or chop the vegetables and noodles, depending on the age of your baby. Leave out the soy sauce to reduce the salt content of the dish.

JEWELLED NOODLES

These noodles are an excellent introduction to curry for children – the creamed coconut diffuses any heat from the spices. Cut the vegetables to resemble the shape of precious jewels, such as rubies and emeralds.

1 Cook the green beans and noodles in plenty of boiling water for 5 minutes, or until tender. Drain well and rinse under cold running water. Drain again and set aside.

2 Heat the oil in a wok or large, heavy-based frying pan. Add the garlic and fry over a moderate heat for 1 minute until softened, but not browned. Add the red pepper and sweetcorn and stir-fry for 5 minutes until tender.

3 Add the curry powder and cook briefly, stirring continuously, then pour in the stock, coconut cream and soy sauce. Stir well and bring to a rolling boil. Reduce the heat and simmer for 8 minutes, stirring occasionally, until reduced and slightly thickened.

4 Mix in the cooked noodles and beans and warm through.

5 Serve the noodles in large shallow bowls, sprinkled with spring onions (if using) and toasted sesame seeds.

Most types of vegetable can be used in this dish. You can add peas, broccoli florets, spinach, carrots or leeks, depending on likes and dislikes. Cubes of marinated and roasted tofu sprinkled over the top make a delicious and nutritious addition, boosting the protein and calcium content of the dish.

75 g fine green beans, sliced into rounds

375 g thick vegetarian noodles

1½ tablespoons sunflower or vegetable oil

2 cloves garlic, finely chopped

1 red pepper, cored, deseeded and cut into small diamond shapes

10 baby sweetcorn, sliced into rounds

1 tablespoon mild curry powder

725 ml hot vegetable stock

200 ml coconut cream

1 tablespoon dark soy sauce

2 spring onions, green part only, finely sliced (optional)

1 tablespoon sesame seeds, toasted

Serves 4

8 MONTHS TO 1 YEAR

Leave out the soy sauce to reduce the salt content of this dish. You may also wish to reduce the quantity of curry powder.

OODLES OF NOODLES

Tofu is highly nutritious and great for a vegetarian diet, as it is a good source of protein. It readily absorbs stronger flavours and is best when marinated and roasted until golden.

FOR THE MARINADE

1 clove garlic, crushed

2 tablespoons soy sauce

1 tablespoon clear honey

2.5 cm piece of fresh ginger, grated

1 tablespoon groundnut or vegetable oil

FOR THE NOODLES

250 g tofu, cubed

25 g unsalted peanuts

250 g thick rice noodles

70 g fine green beans, halved

2 tablespoons groundnut or vegetable oil

1 clove garlic, finely chopped

2 medium carrots, finely shredded

2 spring onions, finely sliced

2 tablespoons Chinese rice vinegar

125 ml water

3 tablespoons tomato ketchup

3 tablespoons soy sauce

55 g beansprouts

1 teaspoon lime juice

1 free-range egg, beaten

Unsalted peanuts, chopped, to serve

Serves 4

1 To make the marinade, mix the garlic, soy sauce, honey, ginger and groundnut or vegetable oil together in a shallow dish.

2 Add the tofu to the marinade and stir gently, making sure it is coated thoroughly. Leave to marinate in the refrigerator for at least 1 hour, turning occasionally.

3 Preheat the oven to 180°C, gas mark 4. Place the peanuts in a baking dish and roast for around 10 minutes. Allow to cool, then place in a plastic bag and crush with a rolling pin. Set aside.

4 Meanwhile, put the tofu in another roasting dish, discarding the marinade. Roast for 20 minutes in the oven, turning occasionally, until slightly crisp and golden.

5 Put the noodles in a large bowl and cover with boiling water. Allow to soak for about 10 minutes until tender. Drain and rinse under cold running water, then set aside. Meanwhile, blanch the green beans by immersing them in boiling water for 2 minutes, until just tender.

6 Five minutes before the tofu is ready, heat a wok, then add the oil, garlic, carrots, spring onions and green beans. Stir-fry over a medium-high heat for 5 minutes until the vegetables are tender. Add the Chinese rice vinegar, water, ketchup and soy sauce and cook for a further 2 minutes.

7 Add the cooked noodles, beansprouts and lime juice and heat through. Add the egg and gradually incorporate it into the noodles, tossing them constantly. Serve the noodles in large round bowls, topped with the tofu and a sprinkling of chopped peanuts.

SPAGHETTI WITH ROASTED BUTTERNUT SQUASH

Butternut squash has a delicious sweetness which is enhanced when roasted. This simple pasta dish is a favourite with children of all ages.

1   Preheat the oven to 200°C, gas mark 6. Toss the butternut squash in half of the olive oil and arrange on a baking tray. Place the rosemary on top of the squash and roast for 25 minutes, turning occasionally, until tender. Remove from the oven and set aside.

2   Meanwhile, cook the spaghetti in plenty of boiling water following the manufacturer's instructions. Drain, reserving 2 tablespoons of the cooking water and return the pasta and water to the pan.

3   When the pasta is cooked, heat the remaining olive oil in a frying pan and fry the garlic for 1 minute until softened, but not browned. Add the garlic and the oil to the pasta with the squash and parsley (if using). Stir well until combined and heat through.

4   Serve the pasta with a sprinkling of the toasted pine nuts and Parmesan.

I small butternut squash, peeled, deseeded and cubed

3 tablespoons olive oil

2 sprigs fresh rosemary

300 g spaghetti

I large clove garlic, finely chopped

I tablespoon parsley, freshly chopped (optional)

40 g pine nuts, toasted, to serve

Vegetarian Parmesan, freshly grated, to serve

Serves 4

6 TO 8 MONTHS
Purée or mash the roasted butternut squash depending on the age of your baby. Make sure the pine nuts are finely ground or chopped.

RAISIN & ALMOND PILAFF

This lightly spiced rice dish is quick to prepare and makes a simple lunch or evening meal. Serve with a green vegetable and top with slices of hard-boiled egg for a protein boost.

1. Put the rice into a saucepan and cover with the water, then bring to the boil. Reduce the heat, cover and simmer for about 15 minutes until the water has been absorbed and the rice is tender. Remove the pan from the heat and leave to stand, covered, for 5 minutes. Leave to cool.

2. Heat the oil and butter in a large frying pan. When the butter has melted, add the garlic, cumin, coriander and cinnamon and cook for 1 minute, stirring continuously.

3. Add the cold rice to the pan, along with the raisins, almonds and chickpeas and stir well to coat them in the spiced butter and oil. Cook for 2 minutes until heated through.

225 g white or brown rice, rinsed

425 ml water

1 tablespoon sunflower oil

20 g butter

1 large clove garlic, finely chopped

1 teaspoon ground cumin

1 teaspoon ground coriander

1 teaspoon ground cinnamon

70 g raisins

40 g flaked almonds, toasted

200 g can chickpeas, rinsed and drained

Serves 4

PAELLA

Paella rice is perfect for young children as it has a soft, melt-in-the-mouth texture.

1. Heat the oil in a large frying pan. Add the onion and fry for 8 minutes, or until softened. Add the pepper and garlic and cook for a further 2 minutes over a medium heat.

2. Add the tomatoes, saffron or turmeric and stock to the pan. Stir in the rice and bring to the boil, stirring frequently. Reduce the heat and simmer for 20 minutes, stirring occasionally, until the rice is tender and the stock has been absorbed.

3. Stir in the peas and sausages and cook for 2 minutes until heated through.

2 tablespoons olive oil

1 onion, diced

1 red pepper, cored, deseeded and diced

2 cloves garlic, finely chopped

2 tomatoes, deseeded and diced

Pinch of saffron or turmeric

650 ml hot vegetable stock

225 g paella rice

70 g frozen peas

3 vegetarian frankfurter sausages, cooked and sliced

Serves 4

6 TO 8 MONTHS

Replace the stock with hot water and omit the sausages. Purée or mash before serving.

RICE & VEGETABLE FRITTERS

This recipe is perfect for using up any leftover rice. Brown rice is a good source of B vitamins and fibre, but you can also use white rice.

1 Mix the rice with the spring onions, red pepper, crushed garlic, egg, cream and flour.

2 Heat enough oil to coat the bottom of a heavy-based frying pan. Place 2 heaped dessertspoons of the rice mixture per fritter into the hot oil and flatten slightly with the back of a spoon. Cook in batches for 3 minutes on each side, until golden. Drain on kitchen paper.

85 g long-grain brown rice, cooked and cooled

2 spring onions, sliced

½ red pepper, diced

1 clove garlic, crushed

1 small free-range egg, beaten

2 tablespoons double cream

2 tablespoons plain flour

Sunflower oil, for frying

Makes 8

BABY VEGETABLE RISOTTO

Risotto is very simple to make but does require stirring time – a perfect job for a little person, as long as you're around to oversee things.

1 Heat the oil and butter in a large, heavy-based saucepan. Add the leeks and courgettes and fry for 5 minutes until tender. Add the oregano and rice and cook for 2 minutes, stirring continuously, until the rice is glossy and slightly translucent.

2 Add the stock a ladleful at a time, stirring continuously. Wait for the stock to be absorbed before adding another ladleful. Continue in this way until the rice is tender and creamy but still retains a little bite – it should take about 25 minutes.

3 Add the petits pois and three-quarters of the Parmesan cheese and stir well. Sprinkle with the remaining Parmesan just before serving.

2 tablespoons olive oil

15 g butter

4 baby leeks, sliced

4 baby courgettes, sliced

1 teaspoon dried oregano

250 g risotto rice

1 litre vegetable stock

55 g petits pois

85 g vegetarian Parmesan cheese, grated

Serves 4

6 TO 8 MONTHS
This risotto is suitable for babies from 6 months, but use water instead of stock and purée until smooth.

... or brown rice, rinsed

425 ml water

1 tablespoon vegetable oil

1 large clove garlic, finely chopped

8 baby corn, sliced into rounds

1 yellow pepper, cored, deseeded and diced

175 g fine green beans, sliced

2.5 cm piece of fresh ginger, peeled and grated

1 teaspoon Chinese five spice

175 g canned pineapple chunks, drained

2 teaspoons soy sauce

Butter, for frying

2 free-range eggs, beaten

Sesame seeds, toasted, to garnish

Spring onions, finely chopped, to garnish (optional)

Serves 4

CHINESE RICE WITH PINEAPPLE

This dish is garnished with strips of omelette, which not only look attractive but also add valuable vitamins and minerals.

1 Put the rice into a saucepan and cover with the water, then bring to the boil. Reduce the heat, cover and simmer for about 15 minutes until the water has been absorbed and the rice is tender. If you are using brown rice, increase the quantity of water by 150 ml and cook the rice for a further 15 minutes. Remove the pan from the heat and leave to stand for 5 minutes.

2 Heat the oil in a wok or large, heavy-based frying pan. Add the garlic, corn, pepper, green beans, ginger and five spice and cook for 8 minutes, stirring and tossing continuously.

3 Add the pineapple, soy sauce and the rice to the wok or pan – you may need to add a little water if the mixture looks too dry. Stir continuously, until the rice has warmed through.

4 To make the omelettes, heat a little butter in a frying pan and pour in half of the beaten egg. Swirl the egg until it covers the base of the pan and cook until it is set. Turn out the omelette on a plate and cover it to keep warm while you use the rest of the beaten egg to make another. Cut the 2 omelettes into thin strips.

5 To serve, spoon the rice onto serving plates, sprinkle with sesame seeds and spring onions (if using) and top with strips of omelette.

6 TO 8 MONTHS
If serving this dish to your baby, leave out the five spice and soy sauce. Blend the rice with a few strips of omelette until it is smooth.

MEXICAN RICE

This nutritious supper dish is delicious with crispy nachos and topped with grated Cheddar cheese. It can also be served in a warm, soft tortilla with a spoonful of guacamole or soured cream.

1 Preheat the oven to 180°C, gas mark 4. Place the rice in a saucepan and cover with water (the water level should be about 2.5 cm above the rice). Add the bouillon powder or stock cube, then bring to the boil. Reduce the heat, cover and simmer for 30 minutes, or until the rice is tender.

2 Add the green beans, carrot, kidney beans, cumin and curry powder (if using) and stir thoroughly. Cook for 5–10 minutes, until all of the water is absorbed. Remove from the heat and leave to stand, covered, for 5 minutes.

3 Meanwhile, place the tomatoes, onion and garlic in a baking dish and spoon over the oil. Toss the vegetables in the oil, until they are thoroughly coated. Roast for 20 minutes, or until the tomatoes are tender. Transfer to a blender or food processor and purée.

4 Add the tomato purée to the rice and stir until it is thoroughly coated. Sprinkle with Cheddar cheese and serve with nacho chips.

175 g brown rice, rinsed

1 teaspoon bouillon powder or ½ vegetable stock cube

55 g fine green beans, sliced

1 large carrot, finely diced

200 g can kidney beans, rinsed and drained

1 teaspoon ground cumin (optional)

½ teaspoon mild curry powder (optional)

6 medium tomatoes, halved and deseeded

1 medium onion, sliced

2 cloves garlic, unpeeled

1 tablespoon olive oil

Vegetarian Cheddar cheese, grated, to serve

Vegetarian nacho chips, to serve

Serves 4

6 TO 8 MONTHS
Omit the spices and bouillon powder if cooking for your baby, and blend the rice until it is smooth. As the rice is high in fibre, combine a small portion with a tomato-based sauce.

TOMATO COUSCOUS & HALLOUMI

Couscous is perfect for little ones – it is easy to eat with a spoon, and can be eaten plain or flavoured with tomatoes or pesto.

1 Put the couscous into a large bowl and cover with the hot stock. Stir well and leave to soak until all the water has been absorbed. When cooked, fluff up with a fork.

2 Heat the butter in a large, heavy-based frying pan. Add the couscous, tomatoes, raisins, pine nuts, sun-dried tomatoes and oil. Stir gently, until the couscous is heated through and coated in the tomato mixture.

3 Meanwhile, heat a griddle pan or grill and cook the halloumi until it begins to colour, but is still quite soft.

4 To serve, sprinkle the couscous with the fresh parsley and top with strips of halloumi. If preferred, the halloumi can be cut into small pieces and stirred into the couscous.

225 g couscous

400 ml hot vegetable stock

25 g butter

125 g canned chopped tomatoes

55 g raisins

40 g pine nuts, toasted

6 sun-dried tomatoes, finely chopped

1 tablespoon extra virgin olive oil

250 g halloumi, cut into thin strips

1 tablespoon fresh parsley, chopped

Serves 4

6 TO 8 MONTHS

If cooking for your baby, leave out the halloumi – it is quite salty, so should only be served in small quantities to young children.

Mediterranean Vegetable Tart

If it's a struggle to get your children to eat vegetables, this delicious tart is the answer, since the roasted vegetables are puréed until they are smooth and creamy.

1 Preheat the oven to 200°C, gas mark 6. Place the squash, garlic, onions and pepper in a roasting dish. Toss in the oil and top with the fresh herbs, then roast for 20 minutes. Remove from the oven and add the tomatoes. Turn the vegetables in the oil and return to the oven for a further 15 minutes.

2 Remove the herbs and discard. Peel the garlic cloves and tomatoes and blend in a food processor with the rest of the vegetables. Leave to cool.

3 Lay the puff pastry on a baking sheet. Brush the edge with egg, then fold over to make a 2 cm lip. Spoon the vegetable mixture over the pastry, leaving a gap around the edge. Sprinkle with the cheese. Brush the folded edge with egg and bake for 20 minutes until the pastry has risen and is golden. Sprinkle with parsley.

4 Cut into slices and serve with potato wedges and a green salad.

450 g butternut squash, peeled, deseeded and cubed

1 bulb garlic, top sliced off

2 medium red onions, quartered

1 red pepper, cored, deseeded and cut into large slices

3 tablespoons olive oil

2 sprigs fresh rosemary

3 sprigs fresh basil

3 medium tomatoes, halved and deseeded

425 g ready-rolled puff pastry

1 free-range egg, beaten, to glaze

55 g vegetarian Cheddar cheese, grated

Parsley, finely chopped, to garnish

Serves 4

6 TO 8 MONTHS
The roasted vegetable purée is perfect for babies over 6 months, but do not add too much garlic. It can be combined with rice and sprinkled with a little grated Cheddar cheese.

CHESTNUT PIES

These attractive pies make an excellent Sunday lunch. Chestnuts contain vitamins, potassium and calcium, making them a nutritious addition to the vegetarian diet. The filling is encased in shortcrust pastry, but puff pastry is just as good, and you could use ready-made.

FOR THE PASTRY

450 g plain flour, sifted, plus extra for dusting

Pinch of salt

225 g butter or margarine, chilled

1 free-range egg yolk

FOR THE FILLING

2 tablespoons olive oil, plus extra for greasing

Knob of butter

1 medium leek, finely chopped

1 large clove garlic, finely chopped

1 medium stick celery, finely chopped

55 g mushrooms, finely chopped

1 medium carrot, grated

1 teaspoon mixed herbs

1 tablespoon fresh rosemary or sage

400 g can whole chestnuts, drained and finely chopped

55 g fresh wholemeal breadcrumbs

1 teaspoon vegetarian Worcestershire sauce

1 free-range egg, beaten

4 tablespoons redcurrant jelly

Milk or beaten free-range egg, for glazing

Serves 6

1 Preheat the oven to 180°C, gas mark 4. To make the pastry, sift the flour and salt into a large bowl. Cut the butter or margarine into small pieces and rub into the flour using your fingertips until it forms coarse crumbs. Mix in the egg yolk using a fork and add enough cold water to form a smooth dough. Knead the dough lightly, then wrap in clingfilm and chill for 30 minutes.

2 Meanwhile, make the chestnut filling. Heat the oil and butter in a large, heavy-based saucepan. Add the leek, garlic and celery and fry, half-covered, for 5 minutes until softened. Add the mushrooms, carrot, mixed herbs and rosemay or sage and cook for a further 5 minutes, stirring occasionally.

3 Remove the pan from the heat and transfer the vegetable mixture to a large bowl. Stir in the chestnuts, breadcrumbs and Worcestershire sauce. Mix well until combined and leave to cool. When cool, mix in the egg.

4 Flour a work surface or board and roll out the pastry. Cut into 6 circles, 12 cm in diameter. Place 2 large tablespoonfuls of chestnut mixture in the centre of each circle and top each with a tablespoonful of redcurrant jelly.

5 Fold in the edges of the pastry to form a diamond shape, leaving the middle open. Brush the edges with milk or egg and crimp each corner to seal. Make 6 pies altogether. You could also cut shapes from any remaining pastry and brush with milk or egg to stick them to the pies to decorate. Place the pies on a greased baking sheet, brush them with milk or egg and bake for 25–30 minutes until golden.

Nut Roast *The chestnut filling also makes a fantastic base for a nut roast. Make the filling following the recipe above adding 55 g mixed chopped nuts. Spoon into a greased loaf tin and bake at 180°C, gas mark 4 for 45–50 minutes.*

8 MONTHS TO 1 YEAR
The chestnut filling is suitable for your baby if puréed or mashed, depending on their age.

Mushroom & Leek Puffs

225 g ready-rolled puff pastry

1 free-range egg, beaten, to glaze

1 large leek, finely chopped

75 g mushrooms, finely chopped

1 teaspoon dried thyme

1 tablespoon olive oil

1 small clove garlic, crushed

4 tablespoons mayonnaise

Serves 4

These puff pastry cases, which can be served as a light summer lunch or supper, can be filled with many different sweet and savoury goodies. Here, they encase a creamy mixture of mushrooms and leeks. If your child dislikes mushrooms, swap them with other vegetables, such as spinach or sweet pepper.

1 Preheat the oven to 200°C, gas mark 6. Divide the sheet of puff pastry into 4 pieces. Place the 4 pieces onto a baking sheet and brush with egg. Bake for 20–25 minutes until risen and golden.

2 Meanwhile, steam the leek for 5–8 minutes until tender. After steaming, squeeze to remove any excess water.

3 While the leek is cooking, fry the mushrooms and thyme in the olive oil for 5 minutes. Combine the mushrooms with the leek.

4 Combine the garlic with the mayonnaise to make the topping.

5   When the pastry is cooked, use a sharp, small knife to cut a rectangle shape into the top of each pastry square, leaving a 1.5 cm border. Carefully lift off the pastry lid and set aside. Scoop out any remnants of pastry to make a hollow inside the box.

6   Fill the pastry boxes with the mushroom and leek mixture. Top with a spoonful of the garlic mayonnaise and replace the pastry lid before serving.

Creamy Mushroom & Leek Puffs Replace the garlic mayonnaise with a sauce made with double cream. Fry the mushrooms in a knob of butter, then add the cooked leeks and 150 ml double cream. Cook for 2–3 minutes until the sauce thickens, then spoon the mixture into the pastry boxes.

VEGGIE BALLS WITH TOMATO SAUCE

Vegetarian mince is both versatile and nutritious. Kids will love these bite-sized balls, served with a smooth tomato sauce. The dish can be served accompanied by steamed green vegetables.

1   Combine the mince, onion, carrot, garlic, breadcrumbs, egg and flour in a bowl. Place the mixture in the refrigerator for 1 hour to firm.

2   To make the tomato sauce, steam the carrot for 2–3 minutes until softened. Heat the oil in a heavy-based saucepan and fry the garlic for 1 minute. Add the tomatoes and sugar (if using) and cook for 15 minutes until reduced and thickened. Add the carrot and heat through. Transfer to a blender or food processor and purée until smooth.

3   Form the mixture into about 15 walnut-sized balls using floured hands. Heat 1 tablespoon of oil in a heavy-based frying pan. Fry the balls in batches for about 10 minutes each batch, turning occasionally, until golden.

4   Reheat the tomato sauce, if necessary, and divide between 4 plates. Top with the balls and serve.

FOR THE VEGGIE BALLS

175 g vegetarian mince, chilled

1 medium onion, grated

1 medium carrot, finely grated

1 clove garlic, crushed

55 g wholemeal breadcrumbs

1 small free-range egg, beaten

1 tablespoon plain flour, plus extra for dusting

Vegetable oil, for frying

FOR THE TOMATO SAUCE

1 medium carrot, finely chopped

1 tablespoon olive oil

1 clove garlic, crushed

400 g can chopped tomatoes

½ teaspoon sugar (optional)

Serves 4

VEGETABLE KEBABS WITH SATAY SAUCE

FOR THE MARINADE

3 tablespoons olive oil

1 tablespoon balsamic vinegar

1 tablespoon honey

FOR THE KEBABS

4 baby courgettes, each cut into 4 chunks

250 g vegetarian halloumi, cut into 16 cubes

½ small orange pepper, cored, deseeded and cut into 8 chunks

8 cherry tomatoes

FOR THE SATAY SAUCE

4 tablespoons crunchy peanut butter

1 tablespoon vegetable oil

1 tablespoon hot water

1 tablespoon soy sauce

1 teaspoon soft light brown sugar

2 tablespoons coconut milk

Serves 4 (Makes 8 kebabs)

Grilled vegetables retain their valuable nutrients which help to boost the immune system and ensure healthy skin, teeth and bones. These kebabs can be served with rice or noodles.

1 Mix the ingredients for the marinade together in a shallow dish.

2 If using wooden skewers, soak them in water for at least 15 minutes before adding the vegetables to prevent them from burning. Arrange the vegetables on the skewers: start with a chunk of courgette, then a cube of halloumi, a chunk of pepper, a tomato, another cube of halloumi, then another chunk of courgette. Repeat until you have made 8 kebabs. Place the kebabs in the marinade, and turn to coat. Leave them in the marinade for at least 30 minutes.

3 Preheat the grill to high and line the grill pan with foil.

4 To make the satay sauce, place all the ingredients in a bowl and stir until thoroughly combined.

5 Place the kebabs under the grill, spoon over the marinade, and cook for about 8–10 minutes, turning occasionally, until tender and browned. Spoon over more marinade if the kebabs look dry. Serve with the satay sauce.

1 YEAR TO 18 MONTHS
Honey is unsuitable for children under 12 months. If serving to young children, remove the skewers before serving.

POTATO ROSTI WITH ROASTED VEGETABLES & TOFU

Many children who refuse to eat steamed or boiled vegetables will happily tuck into them when they are roasted – it enhances their sweetness and gives them a melt-in-the-mouth texture.

1 kg potatoes, peeled

1 bulb fennel, quartered

1 red pepper, cored, deseeded and cut into large slices

2 red onions, quartered

1 bulb garlic, top sliced off

3 medium courgettes, halved and sliced lengthways

4 mushrooms, cut into slices

4 medium tomatoes

3 tablespoons olive oil

Sprig of fresh rosemary

250 g tofu, cubed

FOR THE MARINADE

2 tablespoons soy sauce

1 tablespoon clear honey

2 cloves garlic, chopped

1 teaspoon toasted sesame oil

Serves 4

1   Preheat the oven to 200°C, gas mark 6. Cook the potatoes in boiling water for 10–15 minutes, until almost tender. Drain and set aside to cool.

2   Meanwhile, place all the remaining vegetables in a roasting dish. Add 2 tablespoons of olive oil and toss until the vegetables are coated thoroughly. Place the rosemary on top and roast in the oven for 35–40 minutes, turning occasionally, until the vegetables are tender and slightly blackened in areas.

3   While the vegetables are roasting, make the marinade. Place the soy sauce, honey, garlic and sesame oil in a saucepan and cook over a high heat for 1 minute. Reduce the heat and add the tofu. Stir until the tofu is thoroughly coated. Simmer for 10 minutes, then transfer the tofu and marinade to a roasting dish. Roast in the oven for 20 minutes, turning occasionally, until the tofu is golden.

4   To make the rosti, coarsely grate the potatoes. Take a quarter of the potato and, using your hands, form it into a rough cake shape. Make 3 more cakes with the rest of the potato. Heat 1 tablespoon of oil in a large, heavy-based frying pan and cook the potato cakes in batches for 3–4 minutes on each side until golden (you may need to add more oil).

5   Serve the rosti topped with the roasted vegetables and tofu.

6 TO 8 MONTHS
Leave out the marinade if cooking for a baby under 12 months. Instead, roast a little unmarinated tofu with the vegetables. Purée or mash, depending on the age of your baby.

SPICY VEGETABLE & CHICKPEA PANCAKES

These golden yellow pancakes are made with gram or chickpea flour and make a refreshing change to ordinary pancakes or rice. The mild curry is a good way of introducing young children to spicy flavours.

1 Steam the carrots and cauliflower for 5 minutes until just tender. Cook the potatoes in boiling water for 8 minutes.

2 Heat the oil in a large, heavy-based saucepan. Add the onion and fry over a medium heat for 5 minutes until softened and lightly browned. Add the courgette and cook for a further 5 minutes, then add the garlic, ginger, garam masala and turmeric and cook for a further minute.

3 Pour the stock over the onion mixture and mix in the tomato purée. Cook for 10 minutes until reduced and thickened, stirring occasionally. Add the chickpeas, cooked vegetables and peas, and heat through for 5 minutes.

4 To make the pancakes, put the flour, salt and bicarbonate of soda in a large bowl. Add the water and whisk to make a smooth batter. Leave the batter to stand for 10 minutes. Heat 1 tablespoon of oil in a heavy-based frying pan and add a small ladleful of the batter. Cook the pancake over a medium heat for 3 minutes, then turn over and cook the other side until golden. Make 8 thin pancakes altogether.

5 Place the pancake flat on a serving plate and top with the vegetable and chickpea mixture and a spoonful of natural yogurt.

FOR THE TOPPING

2 medium carrots, sliced

280 g cauliflower, cut into small florets

280 g potatoes, diced

2 tablespoons sunflower or vegetable oil

1 medium onion, finely chopped

1 medium courgette, sliced

2 cloves garlic, finely chopped

2.5 cm piece fresh ginger, grated

1 tablespoon garam masala

1 teaspoon ground turmeric

300 ml vegetable stock

2 tablespoons tomato purée

200 g can chickpeas, rinsed and drained

115 g frozen peas

Natural yogurt, to serve

FOR THE PANCAKES

225 g gram or chickpea flour, sifted

1 teaspoon salt

½ teaspoon bicarbonate of soda

425 ml water

Sunflower or vegetable oil, for frying

Serves 4

6 TO 8 MONTHS
Remove a portion of vegetables for your baby before the spices are added. Purée or mash, depending on their age, with a little hot water.

BAKED BEAN CHILLI WITH TACOS

2 tablespoons olive oil

1 medium onion, finely chopped

1 medium carrot, finely chopped

½ red pepper, deseeded and diced

1 clove garlic, finely chopped

2 bay leaves

1 teaspoon dried oregano

1 teaspoon paprika

½ teaspoon mild chilli powder (optional)

200 ml vegetable stock

2 teaspoons tomato purée

200 g can chopped tomatoes

125 g vegetarian mince

200 g low-salt baked beans

TO SERVE

Lettuce, shredded

8 small taco shells

Soured cream

Cheddar cheese, grated

Serves 4

Baked beans can be incredibly versatile and are delicious in this chilli. Serve in small, child-friendly taco shells.

1 Heat the oil in a large, heavy-based frying pan. Add the onion, carrot, pepper, garlic and bay leaves and cook over a medium heat for 10 minutes, until the vegetables have softened.

2 Add the oregano, paprika, chilli powder (if using), stock, tomato purée and chopped tomatoes and bring to the boil. Reduce the heat and simmer for 5 minutes, stirring occasionally.

3 Mix in the vegetarian mince and continue to simmer for 10 minutes, then add the baked beans. Cook for a further 5 minutes until reduced and thickened. Remove the bay leaves.

4 Place a little shredded lettuce into each taco shell, then spoon in the chilli. Top with a spoonful of soured cream and a sprinkling of Cheddar cheese.

8 MONTHS TO 1 YEAR

Omit the chilli powder and serve with plain boiled rice instead of taco shells.

FUN FINGERS

This vegetarian alternative to fish fingers is great for non-veggie friends invited to tea. This is also a useful way of disguising vegetables if your child dislikes anything remotely green.

1 Cook the potatoes in plenty of boiling water for 10–15 minutes until tender. Add the peas 2 minutes before the end of the cooking time. Drain well and leave to cool.

2 Meanwhile, steam the leek for 5–8 minutes until tender. Squeeze to get rid of any excess water and combine with the potatoes, peas and sweetcorn. Mash well, then leave to cool completely. When the mixture is cool, stir in the cheese.

3 Sprinkle the polenta on a plate until covered. Take 2 large tablespoonfuls of the potato mash and using your hands form it into a 'finger' shape. Roll each finger in the polenta and turn until completely coated. Continue until you have used up all of the potato mixture.

4 Heat 1 tablespoon of oil in a heavy-based frying pan. Cook the fingers in batches for 3 minutes on each side, until heated through and golden (you may need to add more oil). Serve with tomato ketchup.

450 g potatoes, cut into chunks

55 g frozen peas

1 medium leek, finely chopped

85 g canned no-sugar or salt sweetcorn, drained

55 g vegetarian Cheddar cheese, grated

Fine polenta or cornmeal, for coating

Vegetable oil, for frying

Serves 4

6 TO 8 MONTHS
Mash or chop the fingers, depending on the age of your baby.

5 Sweet Treats

KIDS HAVE A NATURALLY SWEET TOOTH, BUT IT'S IMPORTANT THAT IT SHOULD NOT BE OVER-ENCOURAGED. THIS MAY BE EASIER SAID THAN DONE, SO THIS CHAPTER GIVES RECIPES FOR SOME HEALTHIER ALTERNATIVES TO COMMERCIAL PRODUCTS THAT KIDS WILL STILL FIND DELICIOUS.

Coconut Pineapple

20 g butter

1–2 tablespoons maple syrup

200 g fresh pineapple, peeled, cored and cut into bite-size chunks

2 tablespoons desiccated coconut

¼ teaspoon ground mixed spice (optional)

Serves 2–4

This fruity pudding makes a great last-minute treat as it is quick and easy to make. It's delicious with vanilla ice cream.

1   Heat the butter in a heavy-based frying pan until melted.

2   Add the maple syrup and pineapple. Cook for 3 minutes until the fruit begins to caramelise.

3   Add the coconut and mixed spice (if using) and cook for 1 minute, stirring occasionally. Allow to cool slightly before serving.

Tropical Fruit Sticks

Pineapple, mango, banana, papaya or kiwi, cut into bite-size chunks

Maple syrup or clear honey, for brushing

Cinnamon, for dusting (optional)

Serves 2

Children can help to assemble these colourful fruit kebabs, but they do need adult supervision if very young. Serve with a dollop of fromage frais or natural yogurt.

1   Preheat the grill to high and line the grill pan with foil. Arrange the fruit in any order on skewers. If using wood skewers, soak in water for 30 minutes before using to prevent burning.

2   Heat the maple syrup or honey in a small saucepan until runny. Brush liberally over the kebabs using a pastry brush.

3   Grill or barbecue the fruit kebabs for 5–8 minutes, or until the fruit softens and the maple syrup or honey begins to caramelise. The kebabs should only be cooked briefly, to ensure the fruit retains its vitamins. Sprinkle with a little cinnamon (if using) before serving.

Summer Fruit Variation *Any fresh fruits can be used to make these fruit sticks, try a selection of seasonal fruits. Strawberries, oranges, peaches and nectarines work well together, and are a delicious use of summer fruits.*

1 year to 18 months
This recipe is suitable for babies from 1 year, but remove the fruit from the skewers before serving.

ICE CREAM SUNDAE

The combination of ice cream, mango sauce, grated chocolate and toasted nuts will appeal to children and adults alike.

1 To make the mango sauce, purée the fruit in a food processor or blender until smooth.

2 Place a spoonful of the mango sauce in the bottom of a tall glass, top with a scoop of ice cream, then another spoonful of sauce. Place a second scoop of ice cream in the glass and sprinkle with toasted nuts and grated chocolate. Repeat to make one more sundae.

Strawberry Sauce *You can replace the mango sauce with a strawberry sauce, if preferred. Purée 140 g strawberries with 1 tablespoon orange juice and 2 teaspoons caster sugar in a food processor or blender. The strawberry sauce can be served straight away or thickened by cooking over a medium heat for 8–10 minutes.*

1 small mango, peeled, stoned and roughly chopped

4 scoops vanilla ice cream

15 g chopped mixed nuts, toasted, to decorate

Chocolate, grated, to decorate

Serves 2

6 TO 8 MONTHS
The mango sauce is suitable for babies. Serve with a little natural yogurt.

CHOCOLATE ICE CREAM

200 g plain chocolate (about 55 per cent cocoa solids)

300 ml whipping cream

425 g can ready-made custard or carton fresh custard

2 teaspoons vanilla extract

Serves 8

Children always love chocolate desserts and you can't go wrong with this chocolate ice cream. It is simple to make and its rich, creamy flavour tastes great.

1   Put the chocolate in a heatproof bowl and place over a pan of simmering water – do not allow the bottom of the bowl to touch the water. Stir once or twice. When the chocolate has melted, remove from the heat.

2   Meanwhile, whip the cream until it forms soft peaks. Gently fold in the custard, vanilla extract and the chocolate. Stir gently until combined.

3   Transfer the mixture to a 2 litre freezerproof container with a lid and freeze for 2 hours. Remove from the freezer and stir well with a whisk or fork to break up any ice particles. Repeat this twice, breaking up the ice particles each time, then allow to freeze until solid.

4   Remove the ice cream from the freezer about 30 minutes before serving to allow it to soften slightly.

HONEYCOMB ICE CREAM

400 g mascarpone cream

300 g thick natural yogurt

1 tablespoon vanilla extract

6 tablespoons clear honey

2 tablespoons maple syrup

2 honeycomb chocolate bars, broken into small chunks

Serves 8

This light honey and vanilla ice cream, given extra crunch with crispy chunks of honeycomb, is sure to please any child.

1   Whisk together the mascarpone cream and yogurt in a mixing bowl, then stir in the vanilla extract, honey and maple syrup.

2   Pour the mixture into a 2 litre freezerproof container with a lid and freeze for 2 hours. Remove from the freezer and stir well with a whisk or fork to break up any ice particles. Add the honeycomb chocolate bars and stir until they are evenly distributed in the ice cream. Return to the freezer.

3   After 2 hours, stir the ice cream again to break up any ice particles. Repeat this one more time, then leave to freeze until solid.

4   Remove from the freezer about 30 minutes before serving to allow the ice cream to soften slightly.

1 YEAR TO 18 MONTHS
Honey is not recommended for babies under 1 year, due to a small risk of food poisoning. It is also high in sugar.

Juicy Fruit Lolly

Exotic fruit juice is used in this recipe, but you can use any type of juice you like. Slices of fresh fruit add to the appeal for children.

Place a slice of fruit in each lolly mould, then top with the fruit juice. Leave to freeze for 2–3 hours until solid.

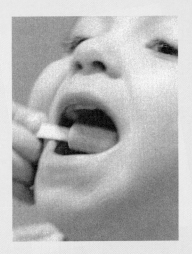

1 YEAR TO 18 MONTHS

You may wish to leave out the fresh fruit pieces if making these lollies for a younger child. Instead of using lolly moulds, you can use an ice cube tray and serve the fruit cubes with a spoon.

2 slices fresh orange, halved

500 ml exotic fruit juice

Makes 4 lollies

Strawberry Yogurt Ice

Children love the creamy texture of these yogurt ices which make a delicious alternative to fruit juice lollies.

1 Place the strawberries and yogurt in a food processor or blender and process until smooth. Stir in the honey.

2 Pour the mixture into moulds and freeze for 2–3 hours until solid.

175 g strawberries, hulled

125 ml thick natural yogurt

2 tablespoons clear honey

Makes 4 lollies

Strawberry & Vanilla Yogurt Ice Cream To make this ice cream, double the quantity of ingredients and add 1 teaspoon of vanilla extract. Follow the method in step 1, adding the vanilla extract with the yogurt, then pour the mixture into a freezerproof container. Freeze for 2 hours, then remove from the freezer. Stir well to break up any ice crystals and return to the freezer. Repeat this process twice more, then leave to freeze until solid.

1 YEAR TO 18 MONTHS

Omit the honey and chop the lolly into a bowl, serving with a spoon.

SUMMER PUDDING

This is a speedy version of the classic summer pudding. The puréed fruit is ideal for children who dislike seeds and lumps.

225 g mixed berries, fresh or frozen

3 tablespoons golden unrefined caster sugar

4 tablespoons water

4 slices day-old white bread, crusts removed

Serves 2

1 Put the berries (reserving a few to decorate), sugar and water into a saucepan and bring to a gentle boil. Reduce the heat and simmer for 5 minutes until the fruit is soft but there is still plenty of juice.

2 Strain the juice from the fruit through a sieve into a bowl. In a separate bowl, press the fruit through the sieve using the back of a spoon – this will make a thick purée. Discard any seeds left in the sieve.

3 Cut the bread into large heart shapes using a pastry cutter – use 4 slices of bread to make 4 heart shapes. (The cutter should use as much of each slice as possible, since the bread loses its shape if it is cut too small.)

4 Place 2 of the hearts in a shallow dish, then spoon over the fruit purée until they are completely covered. Top with the remaining 2 hearts and spoon over the juice. Press down lightly to soak the juice into the bread. Leave for 30 minutes. Decorate with the remaining berries before serving.

6 TO 8 MONTHS
Reserve a portion of puréed berries for your baby and serve with natural yogurt.

PEACH CRUMBLES

This variation of the classic crumble uses whole fruits; if you are just cooking for the children, this makes it easy to make small portions.

2 tablespoons butter, plus extra for greasing

2 peaches, halved and stone removed

25 g plain flour

1 tablespoon porridge oats (optional)

2 tablespoons demerara sugar

Serves 2

1 Preheat the oven to 180°C, gas mark 4. Grease an ovenproof dish and arrange the peach halves in the dish. Add 2 tablespoons of water to the dish to prevent the peach halves becoming dry.

2 Rub the butter into the flour with your fingertips to form coarse breadcrumbs. Stir in the oats (if using) and sugar and mix well.

3 Spoon the crumble mixture over the peaches. Bake for 25 minutes or until the peaches are tender and the crumble slightly crisp.

Autumn Crumbles *Plums, apples, pears or nectarines make delicious alternatives to the peaches. If you have any crumble mixture left over, store it in a container or bag in the freezer for future use.*

6 TO 8 MONTHS
Bake the fruit without the crumble topping and purée or mash depending on your baby's age.

APPLE & APRICOT PUFFS

The topping for these individual fruit puddings is exceedingly light and crumbly. Serve with cream or custard.

FOR THE FRUIT FILLING

Knob of butter, plus extra for greasing

2 medium dessert apples, peeled, cored and cut into small cubes

55 g ready-to-eat dried apricots, cut into small pieces

25 g golden unrefined caster sugar

1 teaspoon ground cinnamon

FOR THE TOPPING

70 g butter

40 g caster sugar

115 g self-raising flour

2 tablespoons single cream

Serves 4

1 Preheat the oven to 180°C, gas mark 4. Grease 4 ramekin dishes. Put the apples, apricots, sugar and cinnamon into a bowl and rub in a knob of butter. Divide the fruit between the ramekins and press down firmly.

2 To make the topping, beat the butter and sugar together until pale and fluffy. Mix in the flour and, as the mixture becomes a bit dry, stir in the cream. Using your hands, form the mixture into a smooth dough. Roll small chunks of the dough into balls and arrange on top of the fruit.

3 Place the ramekin dishes on a baking sheet and bake in the oven for 20–25 minutes until the fruit is tender and the topping is risen and golden.

6 TO 8 MONTHS

Place the fruit mixture in a saucepan with a little water. Bring to the boil, then reduce the heat and simmer, covered, for 8 minutes until tender. Mash or purée depending on the age of your baby and serve combined with natural yogurt.

LITTLE MISS MUFFINS

These double-lemon muffins have a secret gooey lemon centre which remains hidden until they are bitten into. You will need a deep muffin tin and the secret to good, light muffins is to not over-stir the mixture.

1 Preheat the oven to 200°C, gas mark 6. Place 9 large paper cases in a deep muffin tin.

2 Sift together the flour, baking powder and salt in a mixing bowl. Add the sugar and lemon rind and mix together.

3 Place the milk, eggs and melted butter in a separate bowl and whisk until combined. Gradually add this mixture to the flour, stirring gently. Add the lemon juice and mix gently until combined.

4 Spoon a heaped dessertspoon of the muffin mixture into each paper case, then top each one with a teaspoonful of lemon curd. Place more mixture on top of the lemon curd, leaving room for the muffin to rise.

5 Bake for 20 minutes until risen and golden. Serve warm or leave to cool.

Banana muffins *Replace the lemon rind, juice and curd with 2 small, ripe mashed bananas.*

Chocolate muffins *Use 150 g plain chocolate chunks in place of the lemon rind, juice and curd. Sprinkle grated chocolate over the top of the muffins when you remove them from the oven.*

Raspberry muffins *Substitute the lemon rind, juice and curd for 100 g fresh raspberries. You could also try strawberries or blueberries, if preferred.*

Cheese muffins *For savoury muffins, leave out the sugar and replace the lemon rind, juice and curd with 55 g grated vegetarian Cheddar cheese and 2 tablespoons of chives.*

225 g plain flour

1 teaspoon baking powder

Pinch of salt

140 g caster sugar

Rind of 1 lemon

5 tablespoons milk

2 free-range eggs

140 g butter, melted

2 tablespoons lemon juice

9 teaspoons lemon curd

Makes 9 muffins

DOUBLE CHOCOLATE PECAN BROWNIES

200 g butter, plus extra for greasing

200 g good-quality plain chocolate (around 55 per cent cocoa solids)

3 free-range eggs

225 g golden unrefined caster sugar

175 g plain flour, sifted

1 teaspoon baking powder

75 g white chocolate chips

55 g pecan nuts, chopped

Makes 16 brownies

You'll be extremely popular if you make these deliciously light and gooey chocolate brownies. Since they are quite rich, cut them into small squares and serve warm with cream or vanilla ice cream.

1 Preheat the oven to 180°C, gas mark 4. Grease and line a 30 cm × 20 cm baking tin.

2 Put the chocolate and butter in a heatproof bowl placed over a saucepan of simmering water. Heat until melted, stirring once or twice.

3 Meanwhile, mix together the eggs and sugar with a whisk until pale and fluffy. Remove the chocolate from the heat and stir into the egg mixture.

4 Add half of the sifted flour and baking powder and fold in with a spoon, then add the remaining flour and fold in. Add the white chocolate chips and pecan nuts and stir gently until evenly distributed.

5 Pour the mixture into the prepared baking tin and bake for 25 minutes until the brownies have risen but are slightly soft in the centre. Leave to cool for 15 minutes, then cut into 16 squares and remove from the tin.

JAMMY SPLODGERS

115 g butter or margarine, softened, plus extra for greasing

115 g golden unrefined caster sugar

1 free-range egg, beaten

115 g self-raising flour

Pinch of salt

Porridge oats, for coating

10 tablespoons high-fruit, low-sugar strawberry jam

Makes 10 biscuits

A home-made version of the childhood favourite, jammy dodgers.

1 Preheat the oven to 180°C, gas mark 4. Grease 2 large baking sheets.

2 Place the butter or margarine and sugar in a mixing bowl and beat together until pale and fluffy. Add the egg and beat well. Fold in half of the flour and salt, then add the remaining flour and fold in.

3 Place the oats on a plate. Shape the biscuit mixture into 20 walnut-sized balls with your hands, then roll each one in the oats.

4 Place the balls well apart on the prepared baking sheets and flatten slightly with the back of a spoon. Bake for 15–20 minutes until golden. Leave to cool for a few minutes, then sandwich them together with the jam.

CHEWY MUESLI BARS

Dried fruit, oats, nuts and seeds are included in these bars, giving a nutritious combination of vitamins, minerals and essential fatty acids.

1 Preheat the oven to 180°C, gas mark 4. Grease and line a 28 cm × 18 cm baking tin.

2 Place the fruit and water in a saucepan and bring to the boil. Reduce the heat and simmer, covered, for 20 minutes until the fruit is tender and swollen – it should have absorbed most of the water. Purée in a blender or food processor and leave to cool.

3 Meanwhile, mix together the oats, flour, sugar, sunflower seeds and hazelnuts in a large bowl. Cut the butter into small pieces and rub it into the oat mixture using your fingertips until the mixture is soft and crumbly.

4 Spoon half of the oat mixture into the prepared baking tin and press down with your fingers to make a firm, even layer. Spoon the fruit purée over the oat mixture and smooth into an even layer with a palette knife. Top with the rest of the muesli mixture and press down lightly.

5 Bake for 25 minutes until golden, then leave to cool in the tin for 15 minutes. Cut into 16 squares and remove from the tin.

225 g dried ready-to-eat prunes, apricots or dates

250 ml water

115 g porridge oats

115 g self-raising flour

115 g soft light brown sugar

25 g sunflower seeds

40 g hazelnuts, toasted and chopped

115 g butter, softened

Makes 16 squares

GRANOLA COOKIES

These cookies can be made using the granola recipe on page 16. You could also use a commercial crunchy oat cereal.

1 Preheat the oven to 180°C, gas mark 4. Grease 2 large baking sheets.

2 Beat the butter or margarine and sugar together in a bowl until pale and fluffy, then beat in the egg and vanilla extract. Sift in the flour and baking powder and fold in with a spoon. Mix in the granola until evenly distributed.

3 Place spoonfuls of the mixture on the prepared baking sheets and flatten slightly with the back of a spoon. Make sure the cookies are spaced well apart. Bake for 10–12 minutes until golden. Leave to cool for a few minutes, then transfer to a wire rack.

115 g butter or margarine, softened, plus extra for greasing

100 g golden unrefined caster sugar

1 free-range egg, beaten

½ teaspoon vanilla extract

175 g plain flour

½ teaspoon baking powder

85 g granola or crunchy oat cereal

Makes 16 cookies

SCRUNCHY MUNCHY

This crunchy oat and yogurt dessert looks pretty served in layers in a tall glass. Oats, nuts and seeds provide valuable minerals and essential fatty acids, while bio yogurt is beneficial for a healthy digestive system.

1 Place the oats, sunflower seeds and nuts in a dry frying pan and cook for 2 minutes until lightly toasted. Stir in 2 tablespoons of the maple syrup and cook for a further 2 minutes, until the mixture is slightly caramelised and crisp. Transfer to a bowl and allow to cool – the mixture becomes more crispy as it cools.

2 To serve, divide the oat mixture between 2 glasses, leaving a tablespoon to one side to decorate. Stir the remaining maple syrup and the semi-frozen berries into the yogurt. Mix until the berries add a swirl of colour to the yogurt then spoon the mixture over the oats.

3 Sprinkle each serving with the rest of the oat mixture and serve immediately.

Crunchy Oat Topping *You can use the oat mixture on its own as a topping for yogurt or ice cream.*

---

25 g porridge oats

15 g sunflower seeds

15 g pecan nuts, roughly chopped

3 tablespoons maple syrup

125 ml thick natural bio yogurt

55 g frozen mixed berries, semi-defrosted

Serves 2

◆◆◆◆◆◆◆◆◆◆◆◆◆◆◆

6 TO 8 MONTHS
For babies, leave out the maple syrup and oat mixture. Purée the berries and combine with the natural yogurt.

STICKY PUDDINGS

These individual sponge puddings are baked rather than steamed which drastically cuts down on the preparation time.

1   Preheat the oven to 180°C, gas mark 4. Grease 6 small dariole moulds or ramekins and place on a baking sheet.

2   To make the topping, mix the syrup and lemon juice together with a fork.

3   To make the puddings, beat the butter and sugar in a bowl until pale and fluffy. Beat in the eggs, one at a time, whisking the mixture thoroughly after each addition – don't worry if it curdles. Beat in the maple syrup.

4   Add half of the flour and fold in with a metal spoon, then add the rest of the flour and fold in.

5   Place a spoonful of the syrup topping into each mould or ramekin, reserving about half of the mixture to serve. Spoon the sponge mixture over the topping and smooth the top with the back of a teaspoon. Bake for 20 minutes or until the puddings are risen and golden.

6   Remove from the oven and leave for 5 minutes. Heat the remaining syrup mixture until warm. Turn out the sponges into bowls and spoon over the warm syrup.

FOR THE TOPPING

8 tablespoons golden syrup

2 tablespoons lemon juice

FOR THE PUDDINGS

115 g butter, softened, plus extra for greasing

115 g soft light brown sugar

3 free-range eggs

1 tablespoon maple syrup

115 g self-raising flour

Serves 6

PEAR CUSTARD PUDDING

This light custard dessert is similar to clafoutis, the French batter pudding, and is especially delicious served warm.

1 Preheat the oven to 190°C, gas mark 5. Butter a 25 cm baking dish or flan dish and sprinkle the base with 1 tablespoon of the sugar.

2 Dip the sliced pears in the lemon juice to prevent them browning and arrange them in the dish.

3 Place the eggs, cream, milk, salt, flour and remaining caster sugar in a food processor or blender and process until smooth and frothy. Pour over the pears.

4 Bake for 30–35 minutes, until golden – the custard should still be quite wobbly, but it will firm up as it cools. Dust with icing sugar (if using) and serve warm.

Cherry Custard Pudding *To make cherry custard pudding, the classic version of this dessert, replace the pears with 175 g pitted cherries. For other variations, you could replace the pears with 2 dessert apples, peeled cored and sliced, or 4 plums, halved and stoned, or 2 peaches, stoned and sliced.*

Custard Tarts *For custard tarts, put the custard filling in a shortcrust pastry case. To make the pastry, sift together 225 g flour and 75 g icing sugar in a bowl. Rub in 130 g butter with your fingers until the mixture resembles fine breadcrumbs. Add 1 egg and a pinch of salt, then mix to make a smooth dough. Knead lightly and form into a ball which should be wrapped in clingfilm and refrigerated for 30 minutes. Remove from the refrigerator, roll out on a floured surface and use to line a 23 cm loose-bottomed flan tin. Prick the pastry base and chill for 15 minutes. Line the pastry case with non-stick baking paper and baking beans, and bake blind for 10 minutes at 180°C, gas mark 4. Remove the paper and beans and return to the oven for 10 minutes. Prepare the custard filling and pour into the pastry case, then bake at 190°C, gas mark 5 for 30–35 minutes.*

Butter, for greasing

---

85 g golden unrefined caster sugar

---

2 ripe pears, peeled, cored and sliced

Juice of ½ lemon

---

4 free-range eggs

---

300 ml single cream

---

300 ml full-cream milk

Pinch of salt

---

50 g plain flour

Icing sugar, to decorate (optional)

Serves 4–6

AUTUMN FRUIT PIE

Pears, apples and blackberries add an autumnal feel to these individual fruit pies. They are delicious served with warm custard or thick cream.

FOR THE PASTRY

225 g plain flour, sifted, plus extra for dusting

25 g polenta

55 g unrefined caster sugar

Pinch of salt

150 g butter, chilled and cubed, plus extra for greasing

2 tablespoons cold water

1 free-range egg, beaten

FOR THE FILLING

200 g blackberries

3 medium dessert apples, peeled, cored and diced

2 medium pears, peeled, cored and diced

55 g light muscovado sugar

4 tablespoons ground almonds

Makes 4 pies

1 To make the pastry, mix together the flour, polenta, sugar and salt. Rub in the butter using your fingertips until the mixture resembles fine breadcrumbs. Gradually add the water, mixing with your hands to make a soft dough. Wrap the pastry in clingfilm and chill in the refrigerator for an hour.

2 To make the filling, combine the fruit with two-thirds of the sugar.

3 Preheat the oven to 190°C, gas mark 5. Grease 2 large baking sheets.

4 Divide the pastry into 4, then form each piece into a ball. Roll out on a lightly floured work surface until each round is about 20 cm diameter. Place on the prepared baking sheets.

5 Brush each pastry round with beaten egg and sprinkle with the ground almonds. Spoon over the fruit, leaving a 5 cm border. Gather up the pastry to partly cover the filling – the pie should remain open in the centre. Brush with the remaining egg and sprinkle with sugar, then bake for 30 minutes until golden.

6 TO 8 MONTHS

The fruit filling is suitable for babies from 6 months. Cook the fruit mixture separately – you may need to add a little water – then purée or mash and mix with natural yogurt.

TRIFLE TOWERS

This is a departure from the traditional sponge, jelly and custard trifle but it is equally popular with children and even easier to make.

1 Place the cake on 2 serving plates. Put the cream, vanilla and icing sugar in a bowl and whisk until the mixture forms soft peaks.

2 Heat the maple syrup in a heavy-based frying pan, then add the banana. Cook for 2 minutes, turning once, until softened. Leave to cool slightly.

3 Arrange the banana on top of cake slices and spoon over the syrup. Top with the whipped cream and sprinkle with chocolate before serving.

2 slices sponge cake, each 2 cm thick

85 ml whipping cream

½ teaspoon vanilla extract

1 teaspoon icing sugar

2 tablespoons maple syrup

1 banana, sliced

Chocolate, grated, to decorate

Serves 2

GOOEY CHOCOLATE BANANAS

Bananas develop a wonderful melt-in-the-mouth texture when baked, which is an especially delicious treat when combined with gooey chocolate. The bananas can also be barbecued.

Preheat the oven to 180°C, gas mark 4. Make a cut lengthways along each banana, through the skin and into the flesh. Open out the banana and press the chocolate chunks into it. Wrap each banana in foil to make a parcel and bake for 10–15 minutes until the chocolate has melted and the banana is very tender.

Apricot Bananas *Follow the recipe as above, but replace the chocolate with a spoonful of apricot jam.*

2 medium bananas, unpeeled

25 g milk chocolate, broken into small chunks

Serves 2

6 TO 8 MONTHS
The baked banana can be given to babies from 6 months but omit the chocolate.

CARROT CAKE SQUARES

Your child will never guess that this light and moist cake contains healthy vegetables! It has a soft, creamy topping and keeps for up to a week if stored in an airtight container in the fridge.

1 Preheat the oven to 180°C, gas mark 4. Lightly grease a 20 cm square cake tin and line the base with greaseproof paper.

2 Sift the flour, salt, cinnamon and mixed spice into a large mixing bowl. Add the sugar and carrots and mix well.

3 Mix together the eggs and oil in a jug, then pour into the flour mixture, stirring with a wooden spoon until combined.

4 Pour the cake mixture into the prepared tin and bake for 50 minutes, or until a skewer inserted into the centre of the cake comes out clean. Leave for 10 minutes, then carefully turn out the cake and leave to cool.

5 To make the icing, beat the cream cheese, butter and vanilla extract together in a bowl until smooth and creamy. Beat in the icing sugar, then place in the refrigerator for 20 minutes to harden slightly. Spread the icing over the cake and cut it into small squares.

Banana Cake Squares *For banana cake squares, replace the carrots with 3 ripe mashed bananas.*

FOR THE CAKE

Butter, for greasing

225 g self-raising flour

Pinch of salt

1 teaspoon ground cinnamon

1 teaspoon ground mixed spice

225 g light muscovado sugar

225 g carrots, peeled and grated

3 medium free-range eggs, lightly beaten

175 ml sunflower oil

FOR THE ICING

115 g cream cheese

4 tablespoons butter

1 teaspoon vanilla extract

140 g unrefined icing sugar

Makes 1 cake (about 16 squares)

Fruit Soda Bread

This traditional Irish bread is quick to make as it does not require prolonged kneading or rising. Children can help with shaping the bread and, of course, eating it! Serve warm on the day of baking.

1 Preheat the oven to 200°C, gas mark 6. Grease a large baking sheet.

2 Sift the flour, salt and bicarbonate of soda into a large mixing bowl – add any bran left in the sieve. Add the sugar, raisins and prunes, then mix well to combine.

3 Make a well in the centre of the flour mixture and add the egg and buttermilk. Mix with a wooden spoon and then with your hands to form a soft, slightly sticky dough. If the dough is too dry, add a little more buttermilk.

4 Turn the dough out onto a lightly floured work surface and knead until smooth. Form into a round, about 5 cm thick and place on the prepared baking sheet. Dust the loaf with flour.

5 Cut a long, deep cross, almost through to the base of the dough. Bake for 30–35 minutes until risen and golden (the bread should sound hollow when tapped underneath). Transfer to a wire rack to cool.

Butter, for greasing

450 g wholemeal flour, plus extra for dusting

1 teaspoon salt

1 teaspoon bicarbonate of soda

1 heaped tablespoon sugar

85 g raisins

55 g ready-to-eat stoned prunes, finely chopped

1 free-range egg, lightly beaten

300 ml buttermilk

Makes 1 loaf (about 20 slices)

6 TO 8 MONTHS
Serve this bread to babies over 6 months as finger food.

Let's Party

Kids' parties can be a challenge, especially if catering for both veggie and non-veggie guests. This chapter contains a wide variety of fun recipes for sweet and savoury party foods that will appeal to everyone.

MINI PIZZAS

2 tablespoons olive oil

1–2 cloves garlic, crushed

250 ml passata (sieved tomatoes)

1 teaspoon dried oregano

6 white or wholemeal muffins, halved

55 g vegetarian Cheddar cheese, grated

115 g vegetarian mozzarella, sliced

Makes 12 pizzas

Muffins are used as the base for these simple pizzas, but you could also use mini pitta bread, rolls or ciabatta. They are best served warm.

1 Preheat the grill to high. Heat the oil in a saucepan, add the garlic and fry for 1 minute until softened. Add the passata and oregano and cook over a low heat, stirring occasionally, for 12–15 minutes until the sauce has reduced and thickened.

2 Spoon a little of the tomato sauce over each muffin half, then sprinkle with the Cheddar cheese and place a slice of mozzarella on top.

3 Grill for 5–8 minutes until the cheese has melted and is slightly golden.

PIZZA PARTY

Pizzas make great party food and children will love getting involved in the cooking. Prepare the dough in advance, remembering to leave time for proving, and let the party guests try out their creative skills, decorating the tops.

1 Prepare the dough as directed on page 44. While the dough is proving, prepare the tomato sauce as directed on page 44.

2 Preheat the oven to 220°C, gas mark 7. Grease 2 large baking sheets. Knock back the dough using your knuckles, then divide into 4 pieces. To make the pizza bases, form each piece of dough into a round and roll out very thinly.

3 Place 2 pizza bases onto each prepared baking sheet and spoon over the tomato sauce, leaving a border around the edge. Arrange the mozzarella over the tomato sauce, then drizzle with the olive oil. Bake for 10–15 minutes until the base is crisp and golden.

Pizza faces Arrange your choice of topping to resemble a face. You could try slices of olive for eyes, a red pepper mouth and a mushroom nose. Alternatively, flowers, noughts and crosses or animal shapes are equally popular.

Vegetable pizza Supplement the cheese and tomato topping with any combination of vegetables you like, such as sliced red pepper, tomato, mushrooms, olives, red onion, sweetcorn, cooked potato, courgette or aubergine.

Four cheese pizza You could try a combination of cheeses, such as Cheddar, Gruyère, blue cheese and mozzarella.

Potato pizza Supplement the cheese and tomato topping with slices of cooked potato and a little chopped rosemary.

Roasted vegetable pizza Try roasting slices of pepper, aubergine, courgette or onion before arranging them on the pizza.

Garlic bread Omit the topping and smear the dough with garlic butter. Bake in the oven for 10–15 minutes.

THE BASIC RECIPE

1 quantity pizza dough (see recipe page 44)

1 quantity tomato sauce (see recipe page 44)

Vegetable oil, for greasing

150 g vegetarian mozzarella, torn into chunks

1 tablespoon olive oil

Makes 4

8 MONTHS TO 1 YEAR
This pizza is suitable for babies from 8 months, but cut into strips and serve as finger food.

MINI CHEESE SCONES

70 g butter, plus extra for greasing

225 g self-raising flour, plus extra
for dusting

1 teaspoon baking powder

Pinch of salt

55 g vegetarian Cheddar cheese, grated

150 ml milk, plus extra for brushing

Makes 18 scones

*These light, bite-sized scones are best served warm. They are delicious
served on their own, or spread with butter or cream cheese and chives.*

1 Preheat the oven to 220°C, gas mark 7. Grease a large baking sheet.

2 Sift together the flour, baking powder and salt in a mixing bowl. Lightly
rub in the butter with your fingertips until the mixture resembles fine
breadcrumbs. Add the cheese, then the milk, a little at a time, to make a
smooth dough – you may not need all of the milk.

3 Roll out the dough on a lightly floured work surface until it is about 1 cm
thick. Cut out the scones using a 5 cm cutter, re-rolling the dough until all
of it has been used up.

4 Place the scones on the prepared baking sheet and brush with milk. Bake
for 10 minutes until risen and golden. Leave to cool slightly before serving.

CHEESE TWISTS

These light puff pastry sticks just melt in the mouth.

1 Preheat the oven to 200°C, gas mark 6. Lightly grease a large baking sheet.

2 Roll out the pastry slightly, then sprinkle with the Gruyère cheese. Fold the
pastry in half and roll out a little to seal the edges. Cut the pastry into long
1 cm strips, then cut each strip in half and gently twist.

3 Place the cheese twists on the prepared baking sheet and brush with the
beaten egg. Bake for 10–12 minutes until crisp and golden. Leave to cool
on a wire rack before serving.

Butter, for greasing

375 g ready-rolled puff pastry

85 g vegetarian Gruyère cheese, grated

1 free-range egg, beaten, to glaze

Makes 20 twists

HALLOUMI & PINEAPPLE STICKS

This recipe gives a slight twist to traditional cheese and pineapple by using grilled halloumi – kids love the squeaky texture of this traditional sheep's cheese. You can use canned pineapple, if preferred.

250 g vegetarian halloumi, cut into 24 cubes

Small pineapple, peeled

Makes 24 sticks

1 Preheat the grill to high. Lightly grill the halloumi for 2–3 minutes, turning occasionally, until just golden.

2 Slice the pineapple into rings, remove the core and cut into 1 cm chunks.

3 Place a chunk of pineapple on a cocktail stick, then a cube of grilled halloumi, followed by another chunk of pineapple.

VEGGIE ROLLS

Sausage rolls are a must at any kid's party – these veggie rolls are a great alternative which non-vegetarian guests will also enjoy. They are also ideal for a packed lunch.

Vegetable oil, for greasing

1 quantity of vegetable and lentil pâté (see recipe page 48)

55 g mixed chopped nuts, toasted

55 g fresh white or wholemeal breadcrumbs

375 g ready-rolled puff pastry

1 free-range egg, beaten, to glaze

Makes 40 rolls

1 Preheat the oven to 200°C, gas mark 6. Grease a large baking sheet.

2 To make the filling, prepare the vegetable and lentil paté, leave to cool, then mix in the chopped nuts and breadcrumbs.

3 Cut the sheet of pastry into 4 strips, each about 7 cm wide. Spoon the filling down the centre of each strip, then fold the pastry over to encase the filling. Brush the edges with beaten egg and seal well with a fork. Turn each roll over, seam-side down, and brush with the egg. Slice into 4 cm rolls and place on the prepared baking sheet.

4 Prick each roll with a fork and bake for 10 minutes until risen and golden. Transfer to a wire rack to cool. Serve warm or cold.

MELON BOATS

½ melon, such as Cantaloupe or
Charentais, deseeded

6 vegetarian cheese slices

Makes 6 boats

*These melon sailing boats are a simple idea, but make a fun addition
to any party spread. A wide variety of cocktail sticks are available
and paper flags would be appropriate. Watch out for the cocktail
sticks when serving to young children.*

Cut the melon into 6 wedges. Thread the cheese slices onto cocktail sticks
to make 6 sails and stick into each melon slice.

SUNSET JELLY

I packet vegetarian red jelly

I packet vegetarian yellow jelly

Fresh fruit, to decorate

Serves 8

*Most commercial jellies contain animal derived gelatine, but it is now
possible to buy vegetarian alternatives. This recipe combines different
colours of jelly to create an eye-catching sunset effect.*

1 Make the red jelly, following the packet instructions. Pour two-thirds of the
jelly into a large bowl, leaving the remaining third in a jug. Leave to cool
and set.

2 Make up a third of the yellow jelly, following the packet instructions.
Combine with the remaining red jelly, mixing thoroughly to make orange
jelly. Pour on top of the set red jelly. Leave to cool and set.

3 When the orange jelly has set make the rest of the yellow jelly and pour
over the orange jelly. Leave to cool and set, then refrigerate.

4 To serve, turn the jelly out onto a plate and decorate the base with fresh
fruit, such as mango, peach, nectarine and strawberries.

CHOCOLATE FRUIT

Most children love chocolate and combining it with fresh fruit means that they are eating something healthy too. These can be made the day before and stored in an airtight container in the refrigerator.

1 Melt the chocolate and butter in a heatproof bowl placed over a pan of simmering water, stirring occasionally. Make sure the bottom of the bowl does not come into contact with the water.

2 When the chocolate has melted, remove from the heat. Dip the fruit into the mixture, so half of each piece is covered. Place the fruit on a sheet of greaseproof paper and leave the chocolate to harden for a few hours.

100 g milk or plain chocolate, broken into chunks

Small knob of butter

Fresh fruit, such as strawberries, pineapple chunks, clementine segments, apple or pear slices

Serves 10–15

FRUIT GUMS

Dried fruit makes a deliciously chewy alternative to sweets, which often contain non-vegetarian gelatine. You can use any fruit you like – mango, pineapple, figs and pears work especially well.

1 Preheat the oven to 120°C, gas mark ½. Lightly grease a large baking sheet.

2 Place the apricots, apples and lemon juice in a food processor and blend until smooth – this may take a little time. Using a palette knife, spread the mixture over the prepared baking sheet until about ½ cm thick.

3 Place in the oven for about 8 hours until dried. Leave until cool enough to handle, then cut the dried fruit into shapes of your choice.

150 g ready-to-eat dried apricots, roughly chopped

2 medium dessert apples, peeled, cored and roughly chopped

1 tablespoon lemon juice

Makes about 30 fruit gums

CHOCOLATE & CINNAMON SWIRLS

Puff pastry swirls are an attractive idea for a party treat.

Butter, for greasing

200 g ready-rolled puff pastry, about 37 cm × 23 cm

2–3 tablespoons chocolate spread

1 teaspoon ground cinnamon

Milk or beaten free-range egg, to glaze

Makes 12 swirls

1 Preheat the oven to 200°C, gas mark 6. Grease a large baking sheet.

2 Cut the sheet of pastry in half lengthways. Spread a thin layer of chocolate spread on both halves of the pastry, leaving a border around the edge. Sprinkle with the cinnamon.

3 Starting at the short end, tightly roll both sheets of pastry. Brush the top and edges with milk or egg to seal. Chill for 30 minutes.

4 Cut each roll of pastry into 6 rounds, 1 cm thick, and place on the prepared baking sheet. Bake for 20–25 minutes until golden and risen. Transfer to a wire rack to cool. Serve warm or cold.

Savoury swirls Replace the chocolate and cinnamon with a layer of grated Cheddar cheese or cream cheese and yeast extract. Prepare and bake according to steps 3 and 4 above.

ICED CINNAMON HEARTS

Hearts probably appeal more to little girls, but these simple biscuits can be cut into any shape you like. Remember that some cake decorations and types of icing are unsuitable for vegetarians, so check the packaging before buying.

140 g butter, cubed, plus extra for greasing

200 g plain flour, plus extra for dusting

1 teaspoon baking powder

¼ teaspoon salt

1 teaspoon ground cinnamon

115 g soft light brown sugar

2 free-range egg yolks

Coloured writing icing and cake decorations

Makes 12 biscuits

1 Preheat the oven to 180°C, gas mark 4. Grease a large baking sheet.

2 Sift together the flour, baking powder, salt and cinnamon in a large mixing bowl. Rub in the butter using your fingertips until the mixture resembles fine breadcrumbs. Add the sugar and mix well.

3 Add the egg yolks and mix with a fork, and then your hands, to form a stiff dough. Roll the dough out onto a lightly floured work surface until it is about ½ cm thick. Using a heart-shaped cutter, cut the dough to make 12 biscuits and place on the baking sheet, allowing space to spread.

4 Bake for 12–15 minutes until lightly golden. Leave to cool for a few minutes, then transfer to a wire rack. When the biscuits are completely cool, decorate with the writing icing.

GINGERBREAD PEOPLE

55 g butter, plus extra for greasing

175 g plain flour, plus extra for dusting

2 teaspoons ground ginger

½ teaspoon bicarbonate of soda

85 g light soft brown sugar

2 tablespoons golden syrup

1 medium free-range egg, beaten

Coloured writing icing and decorations

Makes 8 gingerbread people (or more depending on the size of the cutter)

A perennial favourite at kids' parties. Children love using their imagination when helping to decorate them.

1 Preheat the oven to 190°C, gas mark 5. Grease a large baking sheet.

2 Sift the flour, ginger and bicarbonate of soda into a large mixing bowl. Rub in the butter using your fingertips until the mixture resembles fine breadcrumbs. Mix in the sugar.

3 Warm the syrup until runny and add to the flour mixture along with the beaten egg. Mix to form a soft dough – if it is too sticky add a little more flour and mix again.

4 Roll the dough out on a lightly floured work surface, then use a cutter to make the gingerbread people. Place on the prepared baking sheet and cook for 10 minutes until just crisp and golden. Transfer to a wire rack to cool.

5 When cool, decorate with coloured writing icing and other decorations.

FANCY FAIRY CAKES

What would a party be without fairy cakes? Children can help to decorate these little sponge cakes, and they'll enjoy licking out the bowl!

1   Preheat the oven to 200°C, gas mark 6. Line a muffin tin with 12 paper cake cases.

2   Mix together the butter, sugar, flour, vanilla extract and eggs in a food processor until light and creamy. (To make the cakes by hand, cream together the butter and sugar, then beat in the eggs and vanilla extract. Fold in the flour.)

3   Spoon the mixture into the paper cases and bake for 15 minutes until risen and golden. Leave to cool.

4   To make the icing, pour the water into a bowl and stir in enough sugar to make a thick paste. Spoon the icing over the top of the cakes and decorate.

FOR THE CAKES

115 g butter, softened

115 g unrefined caster sugar

115 g self-raising flour

¼ teaspoon vanilla extract

2 medium free-range eggs, beaten

FOR THE ICING

2 tablespoons boiling water

Icing sugar

Cake decorations

Makes 12 cakes

CARAMEL NUT POPCORN

Popcorn is exciting to make and a large bowl of it, especially when flavoured with delicious toffee caramel and chopped nuts, always goes down well at a party.

1   Cover the base of a large lidded pan with a thin layer of oil. Heat the oil, then add a thin layer of popping corn, one kernel deep. Cover with the lid and cook over a medium heat, shaking the pan occasionally, until the corn stops popping. Do not remove the lid until the corn has finished popping.

2   Meanwhile, make the caramel coating. Toast the nuts in a dry frying pan until lightly golden and set aside. Pour the maple syrup into the pan and heat. Add the butter and stir until it is melted and the mixture has thickened slightly, then stir in the nuts. Pour the mixture over the popcorn and mix well until it is thoroughly coated.

2 tablespoons sunflower oil

130 g popping corn

25 g chopped mixed nuts

5 tablespoons maple syrup

15 g butter

Makes 1 large bowl

PYRAMID BIRTHDAY CAKE

200 g milk chocolate, broken into chunks

40 g butter

2 tablespoons golden syrup

150 g toasted rice cereal

200 g white chocolate, broken into chunks

Hundreds and thousands, jelly diamonds and candles, to decorate

Serves 12

This is a departure from the conventional sponge birthday cake, but it is easy to make and is always a success.

1 Line 3 baking sheets with greaseproof paper. Melt 175 g of the milk chocolate and 20 g of the butter in a heatproof bowl over a saucepan of simmering water. Make sure the bottom of the bowl does not come into contact with the water. Stir the mixture occasionally and, when melted, mix in 1 tablespoon of the golden syrup. Remove from the heat.

2 Place half the toasted rice cereal in a large bowl and pour in the chocolate mixture, reserving a little to decorate. Mix well, but gently, until the cereal is completely coated. Place 12 heaped dessertspoons of the mixture on to the greaseproof paper to make round mounds. Leave to cool and harden for at least 3 hours or, preferably, overnight.

3 Repeat steps 1 and 2 using 175 g white chocolate and the remaining butter, golden syrup and rice cereal.

4 Melt the remaining milk chocolate and white chocolate together in a heatproof bowl placed over a pan of simmering water. Again, make sure the bowl does not come into contact with the water. Remove from the heat when melted.

5 To make the pyramid, arrange 7 of the milk chocolate crispie balls in a circle on a platter and place 1 white one in the centre. Place spoonfuls of the melted chocolate over the top of the circle, then arrange 6 white chocolate balls on top with 1 in the centre (the melted chocolate will help to stick the balls together). Use 5 milk chocolate balls for the third layer, 3 white chocolate balls for the fourth, and a final single white chocolate ball on top. Leave to set for 2 hours.

6 To serve, drizzle with the remaining milk chocolate sauce. Sprinkle the cake with hundreds and thousands, decorate with jelly diamonds and arrange the candles on top, carefully pressing the holders into the chocolate balls.

7 Drinks

The taste and colour of the drinks featured in this chapter will certainly appeal to kids. They are all easy to prepare and provide great alternatives to commercially produced children's drinks, which can be high in sugar and other additives.

LEMON & ORANGE FIZZ

This vibrant juice is zingy and tangy, as well as being rich in vitamin C. It will keep for 24 hours in the refrigerator.

55 g golden unrefined caster sugar

1 lemon, scrubbed and roughly chopped

3 oranges, scrubbed and roughly chopped

600 ml water

600 ml fizzy water

Serves 8

1 Place half the sugar, lemon and oranges (including the peel) and the still water in a food processor or blender and process for a few minutes until finely chopped and juicy. Press the contents of the processor through a sieve into a bowl. Repeat with the rest of the sugar, fruit and still water.

2 Pour the juice into a jug and dilute with fizzy water just before serving. Add a few ice cubes, if you like.

TROPICAL PUNCH

An exotic combination of pineapple, mango and orange make up this refreshing, vitamin-rich drink.

1 small pineapple, peeled, cored and cut into chunks

1 small mango, peeled, stoned and cut into chunks

425 ml freshly squeezed orange juice

Serves 4

Put the pineapple chunks, mango chunks and orange juice in a food processor or blender and process until smooth (if there are any bits, the juice can be strained through a sieve). Serve immediately.

ORANGE BARLEY WATER

This popular childhood drink is wonderfully refreshing served chilled on a hot day. It's lower in sugar than most commercial alternatives.

225 g pearl barley

1.7 litres water

Grated rind of 1 orange

Grated rind of 1 lemon

40 g unrefined golden caster sugar

Juice of 3 oranges

Serves 10

1 Rinse the barley under cold running water, then place in a large saucepan. Cover with the water and bring to the boil. Reduce the heat and simmer for 30 minutes, skimming off any froth that may appear. Remove the pan from the heat.

2 Add the orange rind, lemon rind and sugar. Stir well until the sugar has dissolved, then leave to cool. Strain, then add the orange juice. Chill before serving.

BANANA & NUT SHAKE

This combination of bananas and nuts is great for kids. Almonds provide many nutrients and bananas are rich in potassium.

1   Process the almonds in a food processor or blender until finely chopped.

2   Add the milk, banana and vanilla to the nuts and blend until creamy.

60 g whole almonds

300 ml milk or water

1 banana

1 teaspoon vanilla extract

Serves 2

STRAWBERRY SHAKE

This colourful and creamy shake is guaranteed to be a real favourite. You could also use raspberries, mango, peaches, plums and nectarines.

Place the strawberries (reserving 1 to decorate), ice cream and milk in a blender and process until smooth and creamy. Serve in a tall glass, decorated with the remaining strawberry.

300 g strawberries, hulled and halved

2 scoops vanilla ice cream

125 ml milk

Serves 2

VANILLA MALT

This American-style shake is thick, creamy and soothingly satisfying.

Blend the milk, malt drink powder and one scoop of vanilla ice cream together in a blender. Pour into a glass and add the remaining scoop of ice cream just before serving

300 ml milk

2 tablespoons malt drink powder

2 small scoops vanilla ice cream

Serves 1

COCONUT & MANGO SMOOTHIE

This smoothie (see left) is similar to an Indian sweet lassi and is surprisingly filling. It is a perfect summer drink.

Place the mango, coconut milk, yogurt, milk, sugar and half the cinnamon in a food processor or blender. Process until smooth and frothy. Pour into 4 glasses and add a few ice cubes. Sprinkle with the remaining cinnamon just before serving.

Coconut & Banana Smoothie *Replace the mango with 1 large banana for an equally delicious smoothie.*

1 large mango, peeled and chopped

400 g can half-fat coconut milk

250 g thick natural yogurt

150 ml milk

2 tablespoons soft light brown sugar

1 teaspoon ground cinnamon

Serves 4

REAL HOT CHOCOLATE

Rich, chocolaty and creamy, this warming drink is a real treat. Use good-quality chocolate for the best flavour.

Gently heat the milk in a small saucepan. Break the chocolate into chunks and add to the milk, reserving a little to decorate. Whisk until the chocolate has melted and the milk is frothy. Pour into a mug and stir in the maple syrup. Grate the remaining chocolate and use to decorate.

225 ml milk

15–25 g dark or milk chocolate, broken into small chunks

½ teaspoon maple syrup

Serves 1

The nutritional information for each recipe refers to a single serving, unless otherwise stated. Optional ingredients are not included. The figures are intended as a guide only. If salt is given as a measured amount in the recipe it has been included in the analysis; if the recipe suggests adding a pinch of salt or seasoning to taste, salt has not been included.

p.12 Breakfast Mail
235 Kcals; 985 Kjoules; 6g protein; 10g fat; 6g saturated fat; 32g carbohydrate; 4g fibre; 1.9mg iron; 460mg sodium

p.12 Eggy Bread
290 Kcals; 1233 Kjoules; 16g protein; 13g fat; 5g saturated fat; 30g carbohydrate; 4g fibre; 3mg iron; 522mg sodium

p.13 Egg Cups
460 Kcals; 1905 Kjoules; 12g protein; 34g fat; 17g saturated fat; 20g carbohydrate; 0.6g fibre; 3mg iron; 560mg sodium

p.14 Melted Chocolate & Banana Croissant
390 Kcals; 8g protein; 20g fat; 8g saturated fat; 47g carbohydrate; 23g sugar; 1.7mg iron; 264mg sodium

p.15 Tropical Fruit Crunch
276 Kcals; 6.5g protein; 9g fat; 3g saturated fat; 35g carbohydrate; 17g sugar; 2.9mg iron; 15mg sodium

p.15 Yoghurt & Banana Munch
335 Kcals; 9g protein; 14.5g fat; 2g saturated fat; 45g carbohydrate; 29g sugar; 1.3mg iron; 93mg sodium

p.16 Golden Granola
340 Kcals; 7g protein; 19g fat; 2g saturated fat; 37g carbohydrate; 20g sugar; 2.9mg iron; 14mg sodium

p.17 Porridge with Apricot Purée
325 Kcals; 11g protein; 9g fat; 3g saturated fat; 54g carbohydrate; 21g sugar; 2.8mg iron; 88mg sodium

p.17 Apricot & Prune Fruit Spread
(per tablespoon) 15 Kcals; 0.3g protein; 0.5g fat; 0g saturated fat; 3.5g carbohydrate; 3.5g sugar; 0.3mg iron; 1mg sodium

p.18 Spiced Apple Purée
210 Kcals; 1g protein; 6g fat; 4g saturated fat; 39g carbohydrate; 39g sugar; 0.3mg iron; 64mg sodium

p.18 American Style Pancakes with Maple Bananas
425 Kcals; 9g protein; 18g fat; 9g saturated fat; 60g carbohydrate; 31g sugar; 1.3mg iron; 431mg sodium

p.19 Sunshine Rice
435 Kcals; 188 Kjoules; 15g protein; 18g fat; 9g saturated fat; 53g carbohydrate; 1g fibre; 4.4mg iron; 199mg sodium

p.20 Breakfast Bubble & Squeak Cakes
230 Kcals; 968 Kjoules; 7g protein; 8g fat; 1g saturated fat; 35g carbohydrate; 3g fibre; 1.6mg iron; 147mg sodium

p.24 Green Giant Soup
140 Kcals; 580 Kjoules; 8g protein; 4g fat; 1g saturated fat; 19g carbohydrate; 4g fibre; 3.4mg iron; 370mg sodium

p.24 Leek Potato & Sweetcorn Chowder
380 Kcals; 1579 Kjoules; 11g protein; 50g fat; 8g saturated fat; 52g carbohydrate; 4g fibre; 2mg iron; 555mg sodium

p.25 Spicy Carrot & Lentil Soup with Garlic Croutons
280 Kcals; 1178 Kjoules; 14g protein; 7g fat; 1g saturated fat; 43g carbohydrate; 5g fibre; 5.5mg iron; 490mg sodium

p.26 Noodle Soup
280 Kcals; 1207 Kjoules; 10g protein; 6g fat; 1.5g saturated fat; 51g carbohydrate; 4g fibre; 2.2mg iron; 629mg sodium

p.27 Cheese & Grape Bruschetta
360 Kcals; 1505 Kjoules; 15g protein; 21g fat; 9g saturated fat; 29g carbohydrate; 1g fibre; 1.22mg iron; 553mg sodium

p.27 Tortilla Parcel
390 Kcals; 1622 Kjoules; 10g protein; 21g fat; 7g saturated fat; 2g carbohydrate; 0.6g fibre; 0.4mg iron; 249mg sodium

p.27 Tortilla Egg Rolls
570 Kcals; 2362 Kjoules; 33g protein; 45g fat; 13g saturated fat; 8g carbohydrate; 1g fibre; 5.4mg iron; 600mg sodium

p.28 Tomato & Egg Nan
300 Kcals; 1248 Kjoules; 13g protein; 16g fat; 2g saturated fat; 30g carbohydrate; 1.5g fibre; 2mg iron; 304mg sodium

p.28 Baby Falafel Burgers
190 Kcals; 794 Kjoules; 6g protein; 14g fat; 2g saturated fat; 11g carbohydrate; 2.5g fibre; 1.3mg iron; 143mg sodium

p.29 Spicy Bean Koftas
70 Kcals; 290 Kjoules; 2g protein; 4.5g fat; 0.5g saturated fat; 5g carbohydrate; 1.5g fibre; 0.6mg iron; 88mg sodium

p.30 Filled Jacket Potatoes
Potato only: 220 Kcals; 920 Kjoules; 5g protein; 6g fat; 0.7g saturated fat; 39g carbohydrate; 3g fibre; 0.9mg iron; 16mg sodium

p.31 Spring Rolls with Sweet Plum Dipping Sauce
100 Kcals; 400 Kjoules; 2g protein; 4.5g fat; 0.5g saturated fat; 12g carbohydrate; 0.7g fibre; 0.3mg iron; 115mg sodium

p.32 Mini Potato, Cheese & Onion Pasties
210 Kcals; 864 Kjoules; 4.5g protein; 13g fat; 2.5g saturated fat; 19g carbohydrate; 0.4g fibre; 0.6mg iron; 191mg sodium

p.34 Humous
123 Kcals; 510 Kjoules; 4g protein; 9g fat; 1g saturated fat; 7g carbohydrate; 2g fibre; 1mg iron; 97mg sodium

p.35 Bean Dip
70 Kcals; 287 Kjoules; 3g protein; 3g fat; 0.4g saturated fat; 8g carbohydrate; 2g fibre; 0.9mg iron; 171mg sodium

p.35 Guacamole
120 Kcals; 490 Kjoules; 1g protein; 11g fat; 2g saturated fat; 2g carbohydrate; 2g fibre; 0.4mg iron; 24mg sodium

p.35 Three Nut Butter
92 Kcals; 380 Kjoules; 2g protein; 9g fat; 1g saturated fat; 1g carbohydrate; 0.5g fibre; 0.5mg iron; 1mg sodium

p.36 Homemade Baked Beans
195 Kcals; 818 Kjoules; 8g protein; 6g fat; 1g saturated fat; 27g carbohydrate; 7g fibre; 3.3mg iron; 602mg sodium

p.36 Sesame Potato Wedges with Garlic Dip
315 Kcals; 1309 Kjoules; 4g protein; 21g fat; 3g saturated fat; 29g carbohydrate; 2g fibre; 0.9mg iron; 113mg sodium

p.37 Honeyed Corn on the Cob
110 Kcals; 451 Kjoules; 1.5g protein; 7g fat; 4g saturated fat; 10g carbohydrate; 0.8g fibre; 0.22mg iron; 57mg sodium

p.38 Crunchy Apple Coleslaw
190 Kcals; 780 Kjoules; 1g protein; 17g fat; 2g saturated fat; 7g carbohydrate; 2g fibre; 0.5mg iron; 45mg sodium

p.38 Country Garden Salad
193 Kcals; 801 Kjoules; 7.5g protein; 16g fat; 6.5g saturated fat; 4g carbohydrate; 1g fibre; 0.7mg iron; 468mg sodium

p.42 Secret Rolls
450 Kcals; 1888 Kjoules; 11g protein; 26g fat; 14g saturated fat; 26g carbohydrate; 2g fibre; 1.4mg iron; 538mg sodium

p.42 Double Deckers
484 Kcals; 2024 Kjoules; 11g protein; 29g fat; 18g saturated fat; 46g carbohydrate; 4g fibre; 2.5mg iron; 807mg sodium

p.43 Pitta Pockets
270 Kcals; 1159 Kjoules; 8g protein; 12g fat; 2g saturated fat; 36g carbohydrate; 2g fibre; 1.5mg iron; 314mg sodium

p.43 Frittata Ciabatta
250 Kcals; 1036 Kjoules; 14g protein; 13g fat; 6g saturated fat; 18g carbohydrate; 2g fibre; 2mg iron; 195mg sodium

p.44 Spinach & Mozzarella Calzone
216 Kcals; 911 Kjoules; 10g protein; 9g fat; 4g saturated fat; 25g carbohydrate; 2g fibre; 1.4mg iron; 549mg sodium

p.46 Bean & Pasta Soup
220 Kcals; 928 Kjoules; 9g protein; 6g fat; 1g saturated fat; 33g carbohydrate; 6g fibre; 2.9mg iron; 656mg sodium

p.46 Melon & Feta Salad
173 Kcals; 721 Kjoules; 7g protein; 13g fat; 6g saturated fat; 7g carbohydrate; 1.5g fibre; 0.5mg iron; 588mg sodium

p.46 Mozzarella & Tomato Salad
150 Kcals; 629 Kjoules; 10g protein; 11g fat; 6g saturated fat; 1.5g carbohydrate; 0.5g fibre; 0.4mg iron; 249mg sodium

p.47 Summer Pasta Salad
450 Kcals; 1891 Kjoules; 9g protein; 17g fat; 3.5g saturated fat; 58g carbohydrate; 4g fibre; 1.8mg iron; 207mg sodium

p.47 Vegetable Crisps
230 Kcals; 972 Kjoules; 2.5g protein; 17g fat; 2g saturated fat; 19g carbohydrate; 3g fibre; 0.6mg iron; 22mg sodium

p.48 Vegetable Sticks with Satay Dip
240 Kcals; 984 Kjoules; 5g protein; 21g fat; 4g saturated fat; 8g carbohydrate; 2g fibre; 0.7mg iron; 267mg sodium

p.48 Vegetable & Lentil Pâté
60 Kcals; 241 Kjoules; 3g protein; 1.5g fat; 0.2g saturated fat; 8g carbohydrate; 1g fibre; 1.1mg iron; 100mg sodium

p.49 Mini Quiches
230 Kcals; 957 Kjoules; 9g protein; 16g fat; 4g saturated fat; 14g carbohydrate; 0g fibre; 1mg iron; 227mg sodium

p.50 Spaghetti Omelette
190 Kcals; 786 Kjoules; 12g protein; 14g fat; 7g saturated fat; 4g carbohydrate; 0g fibre; 1mg iron; 256mg sodium

p.50 Apple Flapjacks
300 Kcals; 4g protein; 13g fat; 7g saturated fat; 44g carbohydrate; 26g sugar; 1.4mg iron; 170mg sodium

p.54 Moussaka
280 Kcals; 1165 Kjoules; 19g protein; 15g fat; 5g saturated fat; 18g carbohydrate; 2g fibre; 2mg iron; 340mg sodium

p.55 Vegetable Hot Pot
400 Kcals; 1685 Kjoules; 15g protein; 20g fat; 5g saturated fat; 42g carbohydrate; 9g fibre; 3.5mg iron; 648mg sodium

p.56 Hearty Goulash with Herby Dumplings
385 Kcals; 1607 Kjoules; 8g protein; 20g fat; 10g saturated fat; 47g carbohydrate; 2g fibre; 1mg iron; 560mg sodium

p.57 Winter Bake
500 Kcals; 2114 Kjoules; 15g protein; 27g fat; 14g saturated fat; 54g carbohydrate; 7g fibre; 3mg iron; 400mg sodium

p.59 Star Casserole
660 Kcals; 2759 Kjoules; 23g protein; 34g fat; 12g saturated fat; 66g carbohydrate; 6g fibre; 3mg iron; 1561mg sodium

p.60 Fresh Pesto & Pea Pasta
720 Kcals; 3015 Kjoules; 22g protein; 38g fat; 7g saturated fat; 76g carbohydrate; 4g fibre; 4mg iron; 211mg sodium

p.61 Creamy Broccoli Pasta Bake
524 Kcals; 2199 Kjoules; 23g protein; 24g fat; 14g saturated fat; 58g carbohydrate; 3g fibre; 2.3mg iron; 514mg sodium

p.62 Tomato & Chickpea Pasta
386 Kcals; 1634 Kjoules; 13g protein; 12g fat; 3g saturated fat; 61g carbohydrate; 5g fibre; 2.4mg iron; 207mg sodium

p. 62 Rainbow Stir-fry with Noodles
311 Kcals; 1314 Kjoules; 10g protein; 9g fat; 2g saturated fat; 51g carbohydrate; 4g fibre; 1.8mg iron; 265mg sodium

p.63 Jewelled Noodles
565 Kcals; 2381 Kjoules; 15g protein; 24g fat; 11g saturated fat; 72g carbohydrate; 5g fibre; 3.8mg iron; 857mg sodium

p.64 Oodles of Noodles
486 Kcals; 2040 Kjoules; 19g protein; 21g fat; 4g saturated fat; 60g carbohydrate; 4g fibre; 3.4mg iron; 1063mg sodium

p.66 Spaghetti with Roasted Butternut Squash
440 Kcals; 1855 Kjoules; 12g protein; 17g fat; 2g saturated fat; 65g carbohydrate; 4g fibre; 3mg iron; 7mg sodium

p.67 Raisin & Almond Pilaf
423 Kcals; 1767 Kjoules; 10g protein; 14g fat; 4g saturated fat; 65g carbohydrate; 3g fibre; 2.4mg iron; 146mg sodium

p.67 Paella
333 Kcals; 1389 Kjoules; 10g protein; 8g fat; 1g saturated fat; 54g carbohydrate; 2.5g fibre; 2.11mg iron; 412mg sodium

p.69 Rice & Vegetable Fritters
120 Kcals; 505 Kjoules; 2g protein; 7g fat; 2g saturated fat; 13g carbohydrate; 0.5g fibre; 0.46mg iron; 13mg sodium

p.69 Baby Vegetable Risotto
433 Kcals; 1804 Kjoules; 16g protein; 17g fat; 7g saturated fat; 54g carbohydrate; 2g fibre; 2.5mg iron; 555mg sodium

p.70 Chinese Rice with Pineapple
330 Kcals; 1378 Kjoules; 10g protein; 8g fat; 2g saturated fat; 54g carbohydrate; 2g fibre; 2.5mg iron; 425mg sodium

p.71 Mexican Rice
270 Kcals; 1158 Kjoules; 8g protein; 5g fat; 0.6g saturated fat; 52g carbohydrate; 6g fibre; 2.6mg iron; 339mg sodium

p.72 Tomato Couscous & Halloumi
507 Kcals; 2110 Kjoules; 16g protein; 32g fat; 13g saturated fat; 41g carbohydrate; 0.7g fibre; 4mg iron; 1336mg sodium

p.73 Mediterranean Vegetable Tart
645 Kcals; 2693 Kjoules; 14g protein; 40g fat; 5g saturated fat; 60g carbohydrate; 4g fibre; 2.8mg iron; 459mg sodium

p.74 Chestnut Pies
759 Kcals; 3178 Kjoules; 8g protein; 39g fat; 22g saturated fat; 94g carbohydrate; 6g fibre; 3mg iron; 411mg sodium

p.76 Mushroom and Leek Puffs
370 Kcals; 1531 Kjoules; 6g protein; 29g fat; 3g saturated fat; 22g carbohydrate; 1g fibre; 1.2mmg iron; 265mg sodium

p.77 Veggie Balls with Tomato Sauce
228 Kcals; 925 Kjoules; 10g protein; 12g fat; 9g saturated fat; 20g carbohydrate; 5g fibre; 1.4mg iron; 245mg sodium

p.78 Vegetable Kebabs with Satay Sauce
408 Kcals; 1692 Kjoules; 15g protein; 33g fat; 13g saturated fat; 12g carbohydrate; 2g fibre; 1.1mg iron; 1171mg sodium

p.80 Potato Rosti with Roasted Vegetables & Tofu
400 Kcals; 1679 Kjoules; 14g protein; 13g fat; 2g saturated fat; 59g carbohydrate; 7g fibre; 3.5mg iron; 465mg sodium

p.81 Spicy Vegetable & Chickpea Pancakes
466 Kcals; 1890 Kjoules; 21g protein; 17g fat; 2g saturated fat; 60g carbohydrate; 13g fibre; 7mg iron; 1112mg sodium

p.82 Baked Bean Chilli with Tacos
154 Kcals; 643 Kjoules; 8g protein; 7g fat; 1g saturated fat; 15g carbohydrate; 5g fibre; 1.2mg iron; 520mg sodium

p.83 Fun Fingers
260 Kcals; 1073 Kjoules; 8g protein; 11g fat; 4g saturated fat; 32g carbohydrate; 3g fibre; 1.4mg iron; 158mg sodium

p.86 Coconut Pineapple
225 Kcals; 1g protein; 18g fat; 13g saturated fat; 16g carbohydrate; 15g sugar; 0.8mg iron; 82mg sodium

p.86 Tropical Fruit Sticks
80 Kcals; 1g protein; 0.4g fat; 0g saturated fat; 17g carbohydrate; 17g sugar; 0.4mg iron; 4mg sodium

p.87 Ice Cream Sundae
330 Kcals; 7g protein; 16g fat; 9g saturated fat; 42g carbohydrate; 38g sugar; 0.8mg iron; 110mg sodium

p.88 Chocolate Ice Cream
333 Kcals; 4g protein;
24g fat; 13g saturated fat;
26g carbohydrate; 22g sugar;
0.65mg iron;
61mg sodium

p.88 Honeycomb Ice Cream
311 Kcals; 4g protein; 25g fat;
15g saturated fat; 19g
carbohydrate; 19g sugar;
0.2mg iron; 183mg sodium

p.89 Juicy Fruit Lolly
60 Kcals; 1g protein; 0g fat;
0g saturated fat; 13g
carbohydrate; 13g sugar;
0.6mg iron; 24mg sodium

p.89 Strawberry Yogurt Ice
73 Kcals; 2g protein; 1g fat;
0.5g saturated fat; 15g
carbohydrate; 15g sugar;
0.26mg iron; 29mg sodium

p.90 Summer Pudding
260 Kcals; 6g protein;
1.3g fat; 0.2g saturated fat;
60g carbohydrate; 31g
sugar; 1.6mg iron;
320mg sodium

p.90 Peach Crumbles
235 Kcals; 2g protein; 12g fat;
8g saturated fat;
31g carbohydrate; 21g sugar;
0.7mg iron; 114mg sodium

p.92 Apple & Apricot Puffs
360 Kcals; 4g protein; 17g fat;
11g saturated fat;
51g carbohydrate; 29g sugar;
1.1mg iron; 149mg sodium

p.93 Little Miss Muffins
317 Kcals; 5g protein; 15g fat;
9g saturated fat; 42g
carbohydrate; 21g sugar;
0.8mg iron; 261mg sodium

**p.94 Double Chocolate Pecan
Brownies**
316 Kcals; 4g protein; 19g fat;
10g saturated fat; 34g
carbohydrate; 25g sugar;
0.97mg iron; 154mg sodium

p.94 Jammy Splodgers
221 Kcals; 2.5g protein; 10g fat;
6g saturated fat; 31g
carbohydrate; 20g sugar;
0.7mg iron; 179mg sodium

p.95 Chewy Muesli Bars
180 Kcals; 2.6g protein; 9g fat;
4g saturated fat;
23g carbohydrate; 12g sugar;
1mg iron; 84mg sodium

p.95 Granola Cookies
153 Kcals; 2g protein; 8g fat;
4g saturated fat;
19g carbohydrate; 7g sugar;
0.5mg iron; 80mg sodium

p.96 Scrunchy Munchy
261 Kcals; 7g protein; 12g fat;
2g saturated fat; 32g
carbohydrate; 20g sugar;
1.6mg iron; 58mg sodium

p.97 Sticky Puddings
430 Kcals; 6g protein; 19g fat;
11g saturated fat; 62g
carbohydrate; 48g sugar;
1.7mg iron; 347mg sodium

p.98 Pear Custard Pudding
444–296 Kcals; 13–9g protein;
24–16g fat; 12–8g saturated fat;
46–31g carbohydrate;
36–24g sugar; 1.7–1.5mg iron;
263–175mg sodium

p.100 Autumn Fruit Pie
761 Kcals; 11g protein; 39g fat;
21g saturated fat; 96g
carbohydrate; 49g sugar;
2.7mg iron; 550mg sodium

p.101 Trifle Towers
350 Kcals; 3g protein; 22g fat;
12g saturated fat; 36g
carbohydrate; 30g sugar;
10.6mg iron; 89mg sodium

**p.101 Gooey Chocolate
Bananas**
161 Kcals; 2g protein; 4g fat;
2g saturated fat;
31g carbohydrate; 28g sugar;
0.5mg iron; 16mg sodium

p.102 Carrot Cake Squares
289 Kcals; 3g protein; 16g fat;
6g saturated fat; 36g
carbohydrate; 25g sugar;
0.7mg iron; 146mg sodium

p.103 Fruit Soda Bread
(per slice) 98 Kcals; 4g protein;
0.9g fat; 0.2g saturated fat;
20g carbohydrate; 6g sugar;
1.15mg iron; 182mg sodium

p.106 Mini Pizzas
150 Kcals; 627 Kjoules;
7g protein; 6g fat; 3g saturated
fat; 18g carbohydrate;
0.7g fibre; 0.7mg iron;
279mg sodium

p.107 Pizza Party
413 Kcals; 1769 Kjoules;
16g protein; 17g fat;
6g saturated fat;
52g carbohydrate; 2.5g fibre;
1.9mg iron; 746mg sodium

p.108 Mini Cheese Scones
88 Kcals; 371 Kjoules;
2g protein; 5g fat; 3g saturated
fat; 10g carbohydrate;
0.4g fibre; 0.27mg iron;
154mg sodium

p.108 Cheese Twists
92 Kcals; 383 Kjoules;
2g protein; 6g fat; 1g saturated
fat; 7g carbohydrate; 0g fibre;
0.24mg iron; 91mg sodium

**p.109 Halloumi & Pineapple
Sticks**
30 Kcals; 130 Kjoules;
2g protein; 2g fat;
1.5g saturated fat;
1.5g carbohydrate; 0.2g fibre;
0.05mg iron; 150mg sodium

p.109 Veggie Rolls
62 Kcals; 243 Kjoules; 1.4g
protein; 3.2g fat; 0.3g saturated
fat; 6g carbohydrate; 0.3g fibre;
0.18mg iron; 59mg sodium

p.110 Melon Boats
61 Kcals; 3g protein; 4g fat;
3g saturated fat;
2g carbohydrate; 2g sugar;
0.2mg iron; 90mg sodium

p.110 Sunset Jelly
122 Kcals; 2.4g protein; 0g fat;
0g saturated fat;
30g carbohydrate; 30g sugar;
0.8mg iron; 10mg sodium

p.111 Chocolate Fruit
64–42 Kcals; 1.2–0.8g protein;
3–2g fat; 2–1.2g saturated fat;
8–5.6g carbohydrate;
8–5.6g sugar; 0.3–0.21mg iron;
14–10mg sodium

p.111 Fruit Gums
111 Kcals; 0.2g protein; 0g fat;
0g saturated fat; 2.5g
carbohydrate; 2.5g sugar;
0.2mg iron; 1mg sodium

**p.112 Chocolate & Cinnamon
Swirls**
76 Kcals; 1g protein; 5g fat;
0.3g saturated fat;
8g carbohydrate; 2g sugar;
0.2mg iron; 53mg sodium

p.112 Iced Cinnamon Hearts
190 Kcals; 2g protein; 10g fat;
6g saturated fat;
23g carbohydrate; 10g sugar;
0.5mg iron; 185mg sodium

p.114 Gingerbread People
190 Kcals; 3g protein; 7g fat;
4g saturated fat;
31g carbohydrate; 14g sugar;
0.75mg iron; 159mg sodium

p.115 Fancy Fairy Cakes
196 Kcals; 2g protein; 9g fat;
5g saturated fat;
28g carbohydrate; 21g sugar;
0.5mg iron; 122mg sodium

p.115 Caramel Nut Popcorn
459 Kcals; 6g protein; 26g fat;
10g saturated fat;
52g carbohydrate; 46g sugar;
1.4mg iron; 194mg sodium

p.116 Pyramid Birthday Cake
261 Kcals; 3.5g protein; 13g fat;
8g saturated fat;
34g carbohydrate; 24g sugar;
1.25mg iron; 232mg sodium

p.120 Lemon & Orange Fizz
30 Kcals; 0g protein; 0g fat;
0g saturated fat; 8g
carbohydrate; 8g sugar;
0mg iron; 0mg sodium

p.120 Tropical Punch
100 Kcals; 1g protein; 0.4g fat;
0g saturated fat;
25g carbohydrate; 25g sugar;
0.7mg iron; 13mg sodium

p.120 Orange Barley Water
20 Kcals; 0g protein; 0g fat;
0g saturated fat;
5.5g carbohydrate; 5.5g sugar;
0.05mg iron; 2mg sodium

p.121 Banana & Nut Shake
330 Kcals; 12g protein; 23g fat;
5g saturated fat;
21g carbohydrate; 19g sugar;
1.1mg iron; 87mg sodium

p.121 Strawberry Shake
200 Kcals; 5g protein; 8g fat;
5g saturated fat;
26g carbohydrate; 25g sugar;
0.7mg iron; 85mg sodium

p.123 Vanilla Malt
428 Kcals; 15g protein; 20g fat;
11g saturated fat;
52g carbohydrate; 43g sugar;
0.66mg iron; 344mg sodium

**p.123 Coconut & Mango
Smoothie**
205 Kcals; 5g protein; 11g fat;
10g saturated fat;
20g carbohydrate; 20g sugar;
1.6mg iron; 287mg sodium

p.123 Real Hot Chocolate
234 Kcals; 8g protein; 13g fat;
8g saturated fat;
22g carbohydrate; 22g sugar;
0.5mg iron; 126mg sodium

Index

Entries in italics denote variations on the main recipe

American-style Pancakes with Maple
   Bananas 18
Apple(s)
   & Apricot Puffs 92
   Flapjacks 50
   Spiced Apple Purée 18
Apricot(s)
   Apple & Apricot Puffs 92
   Bananas 101
   Porridge with Apricot Purée 17
   & Prune Fruit Spread 17
Autumn Fruit Pie 100

Baby Falafal Burgers 28
Baby Vegetable Risotto 69
Baked Bean Chilli with Tacos 82
Banana(s)
   American-style Pancakes with Maple
      Bananas 18
   Apricot Bananas 101
   Cake Squares 102
   Gooey Chocolate Bananas 101
   Melted Chocolate & Banana
      Croissant 14
   Muffins 93
   & Nut Shake 121
   Yogurt & Banana Munch 15
Bean(s)
   Baked Bean Chilli with Tacos 82
   Dip 35
   Homemade Baked Beans 36
   & Pasta Soup 46
   Spicy Bean Koftas 29
Biscuits
   Apple Flapjacks 50
   Chewy Muesli Bars 95
   Chocolate & Cinnamon Swirls 112
   Gingerbread People 114
   Granola Cookies 95
   Iced Cinnamon Hearts 112
   Jammy Splodgers 94
Breads
   Fruit Soda Bread 103
   Garlic Bread 107
Breakfast Bubble & Squeak
   Cakes 20
Breakfast Mail 12

Cakes
   Banana Cake Squares 102
   Banana Muffins 93
   Carrot Cake Squares 102
   Chocolate Muffins 93
   Double Chocolate Pecan Brownies 94
   Fancy Fairy Cakes 115
   Little Miss Muffins 93
   Pyramid Birthday Cake 116
   Raspberry Muffins 93

Caramel Nut Popcorn 115
Carrot Cake Squares 102
Cheese
   & Grape Bruschetta 27
   Halloumi & Pineapple Sticks 109
   Melon & Feta Salad 46
   Mini Cheese Scones 108
   Mozzarella & Tomato Salad 46
   Muffins 93
   Spinach & Mozzarella Calzone 44
   Tomato Couscous & Halloumi 72
   & Tomato Croissant 14
   Tortilla Parcel 27
   Twists 108
Cherry Custard Pudding 98
Chestnut Pies 74
Chewy Muesli Bars 95
Chinese Rice with Pineapple 70
Chocolate
   & Cinnamon Swirls 112
   Double Chocolate Pecan Brownies 94
   Fruit 111
   Gooey Chocolate Bananas 101
   Ice Cream 88
   Melted Chocolate & Banana
      Croissant 14
   Muffins 93
   Real Hot Chocolate 123
Coconut
   & Mango Smoothie 123
   Pineapple 86
Country Garden Salad 38
Cream Cheese & Leek filled Jacket Potatoes 30
Creamy Broccoli Pasta Bake 61
Crunchy Apple Coleslaw 38
Custard Tarts 98

Dips
   Bean Dip 35
   Guacamole 35
   Humous 34
   Vegetable Sticks with Satay Dip 48
Double Chocolate Pecan Brownies 94
Double Deckers 42

Egg(s)
   Egg Cups 13
   Eggy Bread 12
   Frittata Ciabatta 43
   Spaghetti Omelette 50
   Tomato & Egg Nan 28
   Tortilla Egg Rolls 27

Fancy Fairy Cakes 115
Filled Jacket Potatoes 30
   Pesto & Avocado Filling 30
   Humous & Red Pepper Filling 30
   Cream Cheese & Leek Filling 30
Four Cheese Pizza 107
Fresh Pesto & Pea Pasta 60
Frittata Ciabatta 43

Fruit (*see also* individual fruit)
   American-style Pancakes
      with Maple Bananas 18
   Apple & Apricot Puffs 92
   Apple Flapjacks 50
   Apricot & Prune Fruit Spread 17
   Apricot Bananas 101
   Autumn Fruit Pie 100
   Banana & Nut Shake 121
   Banana Cake Squares 102
   Banana Muffins 93
   Cherry Custard Pudding 98
   Chinese Rice with Pineapple 70
   Chocolate Fruit 111
   Coconut & Mango Smoothie 123
   Coconut Pineapple 86
   Gooey Chocolate Bananas 101
   Gums 111
   Halloumi & Pineapple Sticks 109
   Juicy Fruit Lolly 89
   Lemon & Orange Fizz 120
   Little Miss Muffins 93
   Melon & Feta Salad 46
   Melon Boats 110
   Melted Chocolate & Banana
      Croissant 14
   Orange Barley Water 120
   Peach Crumbles 91
   Pear Custard Pudding 98
   Porridge with Apricot Purée 17
   Raspberry Muffins 93
   Soda Bread 103
   Spiced Apple Purée 18
   Strawberry Shake 121
   Strawberry Yogurt Ice 89
   Summer Pudding 90
   Tropical Fruit Crunch 15
   Tropical Fruit Stacks 86
   Tropical Punch 120
   Yogurt & Banana Munch 15
Fun Fingers 83

Garlic Bread 107
Gingerbread People 114
Golden Granola 16
Gooey Chocolate Bananas 101
Granola Cookies 95
Green Giant Soup 24
Guacamole 35

Halloumi & Pineapple Sticks 109
Hearty Goulash with Herby
   Dumplings 56
Homemade Baked Beans 36
Honeycomb Ice Cream 88
Honeyed Corn on the Cob 37
Humous 34
*Humous & Red Pepper filled Jacket
   Potatoes* 30

Ices
   Chocolate Ice Cream 88
   Honeycomb Ice Cream 88
   Ice Cream Sundae 87
   Juicy Fruit Lolly 89
   Strawberry Yogurt Ice 89
Iced Cinnamon Hearts 112

Jammy Splodgers 94
Jewelled Noodles 63
Juicy Fruit Lolly 89

Leek, Potato & Sweetcorn
   Chowder 24
Lemon & Orange Fizz 120
Little Miss Muffins 93
Lunchbox Snacks 50

Mediterranean Vegetable Tart 73
Melon & Feta Salad 46
Melon Boats 110
Melted Chocolate & Banana
   Croissant 14
Mexican Rice 71
Mini Cheese Scones 108
Mini Pizzas 106
Mini Potato, Cheese & Onion
   Pasties 32
Mini Quiches 49
Moussaka 54
Mozzarella & Tomato Salad 46
Muesli
   Chewy Muesli Bars 95
   Golden Granola 16
   Granola Cookies 95
   Tropical Fruit Crunch 15
Mushroom & Leek Puffs 76

Noodles
   Jewelled Noodles 63
   Noodle Soup 26
   Oodles of Noodles 64
   Rainbow Stir-fry with Noodles 62

Oodles of Noodles 64
Orange Barley Water 120

Paella 67
Pasta
   Bean & Pasta Soup 46
   Creamy Broccoli Pasta Bake 61
   Fresh Pesto & Pea Pasta 60
   Spaghetti Omelette 50
   Spaghetti with Roasted
     Butternut Squash 66
   Summer Pasta Salad 47
   Tomato & Chickpea Pasta 62
Pastry
   Apple & Apricot Puffs 92
   Autumn Fruit Pie 100
   Chestnut Pies 74
   Custard Tarts 98
   Mediterranean Vegetable Tart 73
   Mini Potato, Cheese &
     Onion Pasties 32
   Mini Quiches 49
   Mushroom & Leek Puffs 76
   Veggie Rolls 109

Peach Crumbles 91
Pear Custard Pudding 98
Pesto & Avocado filled Jacket Potatoes 30
Pitta Pockets 43
Pizza Party 107
   Four Cheese Pizza 107
   Pizza Faces 107
   Potato Pizza 107
   Roasted Vegetable Pizza 107
   Vegetable Pizza 107
Pizza Faces 107
Porridge with Apricot Purée 17
Potato(es)
   Filled Jacket Potatoes
   Leek, Potato & Sweetcorn Chowder 24
   Pizza 107
   Rosti with Roasted Vegetables
     & Tofu 80
   Sesame Potato Wedges with
     Garlic Dip 36
Pyramid Birthday Cake 116

Rainbow Stir-fry with Noodles 62
Raisin & Almond Pilaff 67
Raspberry Muffins 93
Real Hot Chocolate 123
Rice
   Baby Vegetable Risotto 69
   Chinese Rice with Pineapple 70
   Mexican Rice 71
   Paella 67
   Raisin & Almond Pilaff 67
   Spinach Sunshine Rice 19
   Sunshine Rice 19
   & Vegetable Fritters 69
Roasted Vegetable Pizza 107

Salads
   Crunchy Apple Coleslaw 38
   Country Garden Salad 38
   Melon & Feta Salad 46
   Mozzarella & Tomato Salad 46
   Summer Pasta Salad 47
Sandwich(es)
   Double Deckers 42
   Fillers 51
   Pitta Pockets 43
   Secret Rolls 42
   Scrunchy Munchy 96
Secret Rolls 42
Sesame Potato Wedges with
   Garlic Dip 36
Soups
   Bean & Pasta Soup 46
   Green Giant Soup 24
   Leek, Potato & Sweetcorn Chowder 24
   Noodle Soup 26
   Spicy Carrot & Lentil Soup
     with Garlic Croutons 25
Spaghetti
   Omelette 50
   with Roasted Butternut Squash 66
Spiced Apple Purée 18
Spicy Bean Koftas 29
Spicy Carrot & Lentil Soup
   with Garlic Croutons 25
Spicy Vegetable & Chickpea
   Pancakes 81

Spinach
   & Mozzarella Calzone 44
   Sunshine Rice 19
Spring Rolls with Sweet Plum
   Dipping Sauce 31
Star Casserole 59
Sticky Puddings 97
Strawberry
   Shake 121
   Yogurt Ice 89
Summer Pasta Salad 47
Summer Pudding 90
Sunset Jelly 110
Sunshine Rice 19

Three Nut Butter 35
Tomato(es)
   Cheese & Tomato Croissant 14
   & Chickpea Pasta 62
   Couscous & Halloumi 72
   & Egg Nan 28
   Mozzarella & Tomato Salad 46
   Veggie Balls with Tomato Sauce 77
Tortilla
   Egg Rolls 27
   Parcel 27
Trifle Towers 101
Tropical Fruit Crunch 15
Tropical Fruit Stacks 86
Tropical Punch 120

Vanilla Malt 123
Vegetable (*see also* individual vegetables)
   Crisps 47
   Hot Pot 55
   Kebabs with Satay Sauce 78
   & Lentil Pâté 48
   Pizza 107
   Sticks with Satay Dip 48
Veggie Balls with Tomato Sauce 77
Veggie Rolls 109

Winter Bake 57

Yogurt & Banana Munch 15

ACKNOWLEDGEMENTS

Editorial assistance: Tom Broder
Nutritional analysis: Fiona Hunter
Production: Nigel Reed
IT: Paul Stradling